Legacies

FOR

Libraries

A Practical Guide to Planned Giving

AMY SHERMAN SMITH

MATTHEW D. LEHRER

American Library Association
Chicago and London
2000

While extensive effort has gone into ensuring the reliability of information appearing in this book, the publisher makes no warranty, express or implied, on the accuracy or reliability of the information, and does not assume and hereby disclaims any liability to any person for any loss or damage caused by errors or omissions in this publication.

Text design: Dianne M. Rooney

Composition by the dotted i in Jansen Text and Friz Quadrata using QuarkXPress 4.04 for Macintosh

Printed on 50-pound white offset, a pH-neutral stock, and bound in 10-point coated cover stock by McNaughton & Gunn

The paper used in this publication meets the minimum requirements of American National Standard for Information Sciences—Permanence of Paper for Printed Library Materials, ANSI Z39.48-1992. ∞

Library of Congress Cataloging-in-Publication Data
Smith, Amy Sherman.
    Legacies for libraries : a practical guide to planned giving / Amy Sherman Smith, Matthew D. Lehrer.
      p.   cm.
    Includes bibliographical references and index.
    ISBN 0-8389-0784-9
    1. Libraries—United States—Gifts, legacies. 2. Library fund raising—United States. 3. Deferred giving—United States. I. Lehrer, Matthew D.
    II. Title.
    Z683.2U6 S64 2000
    025.1′1—dc21   00–025923

Printed in the United States of America

04   03   02   01   00   5   4   3   2   1

In honor of

Allie and Weesie

and in memory of

Arne Nixon,

whose greatest gift, planned or otherwise,

was his friendship and trust.

Amy Sherman Smith

———

This book is dedicated to:

my wife, Mimi, and
my children, Dara and Gabriel.

Thank you for your unconditional love.

And to

Marvin Schotland and Carol Karsch,

planned giving professionals and fine teachers.

They helped me to learn the art of planned giving

that I now wish to teach to others.

Matthew D. Lehrer

CONTENTS

6

Advisory Boards *93*

APPENDIX

Planned-Giving Resources *103*

FOREWORD

Approximately three years ago, while I was teaching a two-day module in charitable remainder trusts at the American Institute for Philanthropic Studies, a certificate course sponsored through Cal State Long Beach in Long Beach, California, Amy Smith was one of my students. We quickly became colleagues and friends. It was apparent that she was a "star"; that she would bring great intelligence and insight to the planned giving and development profession—and she has done so.

A few years before that, I met Matt Lehrer while he was working in planned giving and endowment development at the Jewish Community Foundation of Los Angeles. We had a chance to work together. Thus, I got a close-up appreciation of his skills, both technical and personal.

Now they have joined together to write this fine treatise on planned giving, *Legacies for Libraries*, and together have made a wonderful contribution to the literature of planned giving—but with special emphasis on libraries—a part of the educational and philanthropic community that has not previously been served well in this area.

As an attorney working as special counsel to a host of educational, religious, medical, and other charitable institutions and organizations nationally since 1967, I have seen the explosion of the planned giving profession and learned firsthand how important it is to the present and future economic well-being of charitable organizations.

Now those who work for the library community have this valuable resource. Bravo to Amy and Matt.

PHILIP T. TEMPLE

PREFACE

What is planned giving, and why should librarians feel compelled to learn, once again, something new and beyond the discipline of librarianship? Publicly funded institutions must look beyond inadequate state funding. Years of declining public funding have caused libraries to consider outside fund-raising to identify new revenue streams and ensure institutional growth and adequate services. This is not new, but it is challenging.

Victoria Steele and Stephen D. Elder have written the best general book by far on fund-raising for libraries. *Becoming a Fundraiser* is the primer for developing an understanding and appreciation of the profession of fund-raising for libraries. *Legacies for Libraries* springs from the basics of fund-raising discussed by Steele and Elder to address the highly specialized area of fund-raising called planned giving.

Planned giving is a specialized method of raising needed funds. It is a strategy of charitable giving that provides maximum benefit to the donor and the nonprofit organization—in this case, the library. By using financial, tax, and estate planning in formulating charitable gifts, donors can often make larger gifts than they thought possible.

The range of planned giving strategies is vast, from simple bequests to complicated trust arrangements. The motivation of planned giving, however, is philanthropic intent. Donors must want to support the library, and it is up to the development professional—whether a librarian wearing the development hat or a library development director—to recognize that intent from the start or be doomed to frustrating failure.

Our experience includes work as a library development director in an academic library and legal counsel in estate planning and planned giving. Our goal in writing *Legacies for Libraries: A Practical Guide to Planned Giving* is to introduce the principles of planned giving to librarians from all types of libraries so that they can expand their repertoire of fund-raising opportunities. Planned giving is especially helpful in raising long-term funds to ensure the future of our libraries. We hope that librarians will find this book useful and profitable.

About the Legal and Tax Aspects of This Book

This book does not provide a comprehensive treatment of any of the topics covered. Rather, it is intended as a convenient reference on estate and income tax planning and charitable giving.

The book is designed to provide accurate and authoritative information regarding the subject matter covered. It is provided with the understanding that the publisher and authors are not engaged in rendering legal, accounting, or other professional services. Therefore, the contents should not be applied as legal or financial advice.

State laws regarding charitable gifts have not been addressed, although they often conform to federal law. This book also does not take into account the impact of state income taxation and has ignored the various floors and phaseouts connected with changes in annual gross income. The examples use the applicable federal rate for August 1998 (6.8 percent).

Although corporations make substantial charitable contributions and are generally subject to the same rules as individuals, this book focuses on individual charitable giving and does not deal with the specific limitations and rules that apply to C corporations. Because of the pass-through nature of S corporations, partnerships, and limited liability companies, the rules discussed in this book are applicable to charitable contributions made by such entities.

ACKNOWLEDGMENTS

For his support, encouragement, and vision, my most profound thanks go to Michael Gorman, Dean of Library Services, Madden Library, California State University, Fresno. I am also grateful to Phil Temple, my teacher, mentor, and friend. Other friends and colleagues who have supported me, guided me, taught me, and advised me include Diane Miller, Director of Planned Giving, University of California, Riverside; Peter Smits; Linda Frank; all the members of the San Joaquin Valley Planned Gifts Council; and all my colleagues in ALADN and on LIBDEV. Special thanks to my colleagues at Bowling Green State University Library, the University of Louisville Library, and the University of Florida Libraries, who so generously provided excellent examples for this book. For their friendship and support and for making library development so much fun, I thank Irene Hoffman and Leslie Dibona.

—AMY SHERMAN SMITH

For lending their expertise and time to review this manuscript, I would like to thank the following individuals: D. Stephen Boner, a San Diego estate planning expert and my first employer; my long-standing and best friend of some seventeen years, David Gould, an economist with the Federal Reserve Bank in Dallas, who was actually able to explain to me in understandable terms why bond prices generally move in the opposite direction of prevailing market interest rates. I, in turn, will share this wisdom with you, the reader. I would also like to thank my parents, Cy and Sheila Lehrer, for their assistance in editing this manuscript.

—MATTHEW LEHRER

1

Planned Giving
for Libraries

One universal fact of life for libraries, regardless of type, is inadequate funding. Librarians well know the financial conundrum of library economics: increasing costs of materials, increasing costs of new technology, and decreasing funds to pay for them. For some, costs for new technology have usurped funds for books. Like Alice, it takes all the running we can do to stay in the same place. The only solution is to seek funds beyond the limitations of state funding.

Libraries—and librarians—are forced to raise funds. Private academic libraries have led the charge. Most private institutions have a tradition of fund-raising, and, in some cases, that has spilled over to the libraries as well. Academic libraries in public universities have joined the fray, and more and more public libraries are coming on board with fund-raising efforts.

The first organization formed specifically for academic library fund-raising was Development Officers of Research Academic Libraries (DORAL) in 1987. Academic Library Advancement and Development Network (ALADN) was formed in 1995 and has grown enormously. Unlike DORAL, ALADN has an open membership and includes many development directors from public universities. ALADN is comprised of both fund-raising professionals working in academic libraries and librarians wearing the fund-raising development hat.

The American Library Association has begun to recognize fund-raising as a pertinent area of librarianship. The Library Administration and Management Association now includes fund-raising development. Many regional library organizations, such as the California Library

Association, have added fund-raising development to their convention programs.

In a recent national survey of academic library development, colleagues Irene Hoffman at Cal Poly San Luis Obispo, Leslie DiBona at San Diego State University, and Amy Sherman Smith found that most academic library development programs are less than five years old. The programs that have been around the longest are primarily from private universities and colleges.

Libraries are competing with a multitude of other institutions and charities at a time when the face of charitable giving is changing. In the 1994 issue of *Fund Raising Management*, Jerold Panas wrote of the future of fund-raising: "Foundation giving may increase slightly, corporate gifts will decline, and government funding will cease. But the most important will be the generation of large gifts from individuals."[1]

The greatest change in fund-raising will be over the next twenty years when the largest transgenerational transfer of wealth in history will occur. Estimates are that many trillions of dollars will move from one generation to the next, with a significant portion potentially lost to transfer taxes.

Fund-raisers enthusiastically applaud the very public pledge of $1 billion by philanthropist Ted Turner and his public exhortation to his fellow billionaires to become generous philanthropists.

Another very public pledge by Microsoft's Bill Gates benefits public libraries. Hailed as the new Carnegie, Gates is donating equipment and software to public libraries so that impoverished areas can have access to the Internet (and to Microsoft). While the donation is greatly appreciated, it does not do much to help with the materials and service concerns of most libraries now or in the future.

Libraries and librarians must begin to think creatively about the future of our libraries. Planned giving presents many options for future funding and complements annual giving and major gifts fund-raising efforts.

Basic Fund-Raising

In an effort to demystify fund-raising as completely as possible, it might be helpful to cover some fundamental fund-raising concepts.

Case Statement

The first step in developing a fund-raising strategy is to articulate the mission of your library and your needs and to develop a case statement. The mission statement is what you do and whom you serve. It is the statement that articulates your uniqueness as an institution. The case statement is your statement of needs—why you are involved in a fund-raising effort.

The case statement represents the core of the fund-raising purpose, and it will become your raison d'être when you are wearing your fund-raising hat. The document will also be useful as literature to leave with a donor considering a proposal.

Library development, like all fund-raising development, is about values and relationships. This is the core. Donors give because they value your institution and because they have a relationship with you as the facilitator of their philanthropic vision. Remember that donors usually have more than one philanthropic interest, but also keep in mind that you are not competing. Your library is part of the donor's value system, and your relationship, built on trust and shared values, is what will facilitate the coming together of your institution's vision with your donor's vision.

Prospects

Identifying prospects is another foundation platform of your development program. This process is described in greater detail later in this book, but essentially it is finding who your potential donors are. Apparent ability to give is only part of the equation, so identifying potential donors is more than just "She's rich! Ergo, she'll give to my library!"

Cultivating prospects is the process leading up to the presentation of a proposal. The cultivation process is the building of the relationship with the donor over time to build trust and to establish a congruence of values. Important information is gleaned during the cultivation period: ability to give; desire to give; family responsibilities; reasons for giving, which are helpful when presenting recognition opportunities; and other pertinent information that will help you decide to solicit a gift.

Before prospects are qualified, they are suspects. An ideal scenario is that a suspect—maybe a member of your Friends group—becomes a prospect when, for example, in conversation you learn that this person is a wealthy widow with no heirs, and she tells you how much she values your library. When this same prospect tells you she would like to do something to enhance your business collection as a memorial to her deceased husband, then you have a donor.

Proposals

In this last scenario, the prospect presented her desire to help the library. But in some cases, you will need to make the solicitation—that is, you will ask the prospect to become a donor by making a proposal. Remember that this step comes after you have established that the prospect has the interest and the means to make a donation and after you have cultivated a relationship. At this point, you may find it surprisingly easy to say, "Mabel, would you consider supporting the library by making a gift to enhance our business collection? Perhaps this could be a memorial gift in honor of your late husband."

Always have a written proposal to leave behind—one that is simple and short (one page). You might make the heading in the name of the gift, for example, "The George Jones Endowment for Business," which brings the concept alive.

Ways of Giving

Donors give in different ways. They can give cash, property, stock, tangible personal property, and, of course, collections of books. The ramifications of these ways of giving are explained in greater detail later in this book, as different kinds of gifts incur different tax considerations.

Donors give at different levels. Donations can be classified as annual gifts, major gifts, and planned gifts. Annual gifts are generated perhaps in response to your annual giving program. Usually, these gifts are small and spontaneous, in that donors just write a check and send it off without consulting financial or tax planners.

Annual Gifts

Annual gifts usually go for unrestricted purposes, although some sophisticated donors may indicate that they want their annual donation to go for a specific purpose.

Major Gifts

Major gifts are altogether different from annual gifts. Major gifts usually represent a larger financial commitment and a longer consideration process. They are usually restricted to some specific purpose and can be in the form of a planned gift. In the true sense, a major gift is always a planned gift. Another name for a major gift is a "stop-and-think gift."

Planned Gifts

A planned gift is the method for making a major gift. Some major gifts are outright: either cash or assets. Planned gifts are those that come in forms other than outright cash or assets and instead are in trust form or bequests. Gifts of real estate, life insurance, and pension plans are considered planned gifts and are, as well, major gifts. Perhaps it is fair to say that planned gifts are the more complicated major gifts.

Endowments

The term *planned gift* is often mistakenly used interchangeably with *endowment gift*. To clear up the confusion, endowments are funds established with a specific purpose from which only the interest from the corpus is used. This ensures the gift will continue in perpetuity, unlike a donation that is used up over time.

The Madden Library at the California University, Fresno, received a donation from the university basketball coach and his wife to establish the Jerry and Lois Tarkanian Book Fund. It was not established as an endowment, and when the Library has spent all the money in the fund, the gift is finished. If the couple had established an endowment to purchase books, then the interest from the endowment fund would be used to purchase books and the fund would continue, generating funds from which to buy books in perpetuity.

In this case, the Tarkanians saw an opportunity to partner the university basketball program with the library in a fund-raising program called Baskets for Books, in which a corporate or business sponsor pledges a dollar for every point the basketball team scores during the season. At the end of the season, that amount is donated to the Jerry and Lois Tarkanian Book Fund. As long as the basketball team scores points and as long as there are sponsors, the Tarkanian Book Fund should have funds.

Many institutions require minimum amounts to establish an endowment. Remember, there has to be enough to generate interest with which the library can purchase materials. In some cases, institutions offer quasi-endowment opportunities. These quasi endowments work on the same principle as regular endowments, but they are established with less money than ordinarily required for an endowment. These quasi-endowments benefit from added donations that grow them into regular endowments.

At the library of the University of California, Riverside, $10,000 is the minimum required to establish an endowment. At 4 percent, the interest generated annually is $400. Also, keep in mind that depending on where you house the endowment, there will probably be fees associated with the management of the endowment fund. Also, different institutions have different investment policies that will affect the amount paid in interest. Even in a bull market where earning may be as high as 10 percent annually, some institutions take a very conservative approach and only pay out 4 percent. The rest of the earnings are put back into the corpus of the endowment fund, and the following year, the 4 percent payout is from the initial amount plus the 6 percent realized but not paid out from the previous year. This is called *total return*.

Endowments provide wonderful naming opportunities for your donors. As in the example above, Mabel Jones can memorialize her husband by naming the endowment for him. Capital campaign fundraising also provides many naming opportunities. The library at Pasadena City College is a wonderful example of a collage of naming opportunities—the library itself is named and many rooms inside the library are named for generous donors.

Capital Campaigns

Capital campaigns are fund-raising campaigns restricted to a specific period of time and usually for specific purposes as well. For example, a capital campaign can be for a building project, but such campaigns often include more than one purpose and can include components for endowments and programs. In academic libraries, campaigns are often part of a university-wide campaign and the library identifies its needs as a component of the larger campaign. Capital campaigns generate much enthusiasm and support, and university libraries should make sure they are included in a university-wide campaign.

Library Prospects

Who are your library's prospects? We would include previous donors, trustees, volunteer leaders, Friends, retired board volunteers, retired and current faculty and staff, program and special event attendees, and members of your advisory board.

Previous Donors

If your library has kept records of past donations, consider the list your prospect pool. Note especially those donors who have given regularly over time, as well as those who have given large donations. If you are new to the library and are not familiar with the names on the list, consult with staff and faculty who may be helpful in identifying the donors and filling you in on important historical information.

Trustees and Volunteers

Trustees and volunteer board members have already identified themselves as supporters of your library. Often trustees and board members are in the preferred planned-giving prospect range, due to their age and involvement in your library. They may also meet the financial criteria (ability to give) for planned-giving prospects.

Friends of the Library

Of course, your Friends group is an excellent pool of planned-giving prospects. Friends are self-identified as interested in your library. If your Friends group is part of an annual giving program, they are already donors to your library. There is some controversy in the profession, especially in academic libraries, about whether Friends groups are worth the effort. For planned giving purposes, Friends groups are an excellent source of self-identified and usually age-appropriate supporters of your library. Friends groups are most effective as part of an annual giving program rather than as a membership organization, the latter meaning that a member would pay a fee to join and receive in return certain privileges, including invitations to events, borrowing privileges (relevant for academic libraries, not public libraries), and other premiums. As part of an annual giving program, anyone who gives to the library is a Friend. If you wish to begin a Friends group, I would strongly suggest you implement it as an annual giving program. If you already have a membership Friends program, you should think about making a transition to an annual giving program.

Staff and Faculty

Retired and current staff and faculty should also be considered strong planned-giving prospects. They have a relationship with the library, and if they are unmarried with no children, they may well consider the library in their estate plans.

Program Attendees

Guests who have attended programs and special events hosted by your library have therefore shown an interest and should be considered prospects. Depending on their age and circumstance, they may well be strong planned-giving prospects. It is helpful when planning events to have attendees RSVP so that you have a list of those who attended. For events and programs that are not by invitation, it is helpful to have a sign-in sheet (with addresses) so that you capture that information. As a librarian wearing the development hat, it is imperative that you attend library events and programs and circulate among the guests.

Identifying Prospects

What are some of the characteristics of a good planned-giving prospect? The ideal and stereotypical planned-giving prospect is a wealthy widow, over seventy, with no direct heirs. Maybe you have some Friends members and volunteers who match this description. However, there are other planned-giving profiles you should recognize in your prospect pool.

Age should be considered in identifying planned-giving prospects. Planned-giving experts generally agree that donors fifty-five years old and older are the best planned-giving prospects. There are many reasons for this demarcation, although this does not rule out younger prospects in some cases.

Donors fifty-five to sixty-five years old, while still in the wealth-accumulation stage of their financial life, are also thinking more about estate planning and the disposition of their financial assets. These prospects are interested in information about wills, trusts, probate, investment opportunities for retirement funds, gifting techniques, and transfer taxes. They are also concerned about their long-term financial and physical health, with special attention to planning well so as not to outlive their assets.

Donors sixty-five to seventy-five are probably finished with the ac-cumulation stage of their financial life and are more interested in the conservation and preservation of their estate assets. Most planned gifts come through wills or other estate plans at death, and this group may have considered the distribution of their assets when they no longer need them. This particular age group may also be interested in planned-giving vehicles that provide a steady life income, such as gift annuities.

Donors older than seventy-five may have different concerns. It is interesting to note that this particular age group is and will continue to be dominated by women. Eighty percent of women over age seventy-five live alone.[2] This group may also be the wealthiest, due in large part to investment returns of the bull stock market. However, wealth notwithstanding, this group of donors is still concerned about outliving assets and living comfortably until death. For them, life income vehi-cles are attractive. For the donor with limited assets, bequest planning may be more appropriate.

Donors without heirs should be considered ideal planned-giving prospects. These donors are not concerned about leaving assets to chil-dren or grandchildren and may well leave their estate to the charities and institutions that have meant much to them during their lifetime.

Younger donors should not necessarily be overlooked. A deferred-gift annuity, explained in chapter 3, is an ideal planned-giving vehicle for younger donors. A colleague of Amy Sherman Smith, Irene Hoffman, tells of a rancher in her community who set up charitable gift annuities for his ranch workers—a very creative way to donate as-sets in the future while addressing practical concerns first.

Donors with children should not be overlooked. Some parents are concerned about leaving too much too soon to their children and thereby stifling their incentive. Donors often share such information during the cultivation period.

Wealth is not always apparent, and therefore should not be the de-termining factor in prospecting for planned-giving donors. The record of involvement in your library is a much better indicator of philan-thropic intent. Donors who have given consistently, even small amounts of money, over many years have identified themselves as people inter-ested in the institution and willing to support it. In addition, volunteers who have given their time show support and interest in your library as well. These are self-identified planned-giving prospects.

Commitment to and affiliation with your library are major factors in identifying planned-giving prospects. The consistent donors, volunteers, and others with a relationship to your library, regardless of apparent wealth, should be cultivated for planned gifts.

Environmental trends in charitable giving over the years show that women will be giving more. One reason is that women outlive men and are, more and more, in control of great wealth. Much literature is coming out about the philanthropic trends of women donors. Some of these include *Reinventing Fundraising: Realizing the Potential of Women's Philanthropy* by Sondra C. Shaw and Martha A. Taylor; *Women and Philanthropy: Old Stereotypes and New Challenges*, by Mary Ellen J. Capek, and *Cultures of Giving II: How Heritage, Gender, Wealth, and Values Influence Philanthropy*, by Charles H. Hamilton and Warren Ilchman.

Organizations for women and philanthropy include Women and Philanthropy (http://www.womenphil.org), UCLA Women and Philanthropy (http://women.support.ucla.edu), and Women's Philanthropy Institute (http://www.women-philanthropy.org).

Other relevant indicators for planned-giving prospects include marital status and children. As mentioned before, those individuals without heirs—either a spouse or children—are traditionally the best planned-giving prospects.

Philanthropic Intent

Philanthropic intent cannot be underestimated as a highly important factor in determining a solid planned-giving prospect. Past giving level is also indicative of a good prospect. As planned giving moves more and more to the forefront as a charitable giving tool, there are bound to be donors who are really more interested in the avoidance of taxes than in making philanthropic gifts. In some cases, this might even work for your library, but overall, really successful planned gifts are made because of philanthropic intent to support the mission of your institution.

A case in point regarding this aspect of planned giving occurred at our library. An older couple, with five grown children and a very loose affiliation to the university in general, and the library in particular, decided on the advice of their estate attorney to set up a charitable remainder trust to benefit the library. The asset used to fund the trust was a piece of property out in the north of town where there is great potential for future development.

The trust was established; the asset was valued at $1 million and there was much celebration on campus and in the library. The special collection library was renamed in their honor. Three years later, the trustee has still not been able to sell the land. The initial valuation, it seems, was greatly inflated, and when the trust "matures" the actual gift will be considerably less than first announced. The flaw was moving too quickly, jumping on the opportunity, and the seemingly "win-win" scenario of the establishment of the trust. However, the donor's intent was to get rid of land they could not sell and to get a tax deduction for the charitable gift. At some point, the library will benefit from the gift, but not to the tune of $1 million.

Importance of Asking

While philanthropic intent and prior giving history are strong indicators for good planned-giving prospects, the timeliness of asking—or the asking itself—is the single most important aspect of successful planned giving. In fund-raising, if you don't ask, you don't get. The same is true for planned giving. You must educate your prospects about planned giving if you want them to consider making a planned gift. Let your prospects know of the possibilities, and, when the time comes, ask them to consider your library in their estate or charitable giving plans.

This is the part that may well strike fear in the hearts of librarians—the asking—but if you have considered the best planned-giving prospects and cultivated them, it may well be less scary than you imagine. The beauty of planned giving is that it often rewards the donor as much as the library, and presenting the information to the prospects enables them to fulfill their charitable desires to help your library. Instead of focusing on the fear of asking for money or worse yet, discussing mortality issues, consider yourself to be the facilitator for helping donors to leave a legacy to an institution close to their hearts.

In conclusion, look to your Friends, previous donors, trustees, retired board members, current and retired faculty and staff, program attendees, and volunteers. They are a rich resource of planned-giving opportunities. Remember the factors that indicate potential success in any planned-giving program: age, commitment to or affiliation with your library, gender, marital status, children, philanthropic intent, past support, and asking.

The Low-Budget Planned-Giving Initiative

What does a librarian need to know about planned giving and how can libraries possibly expect to fund another fund-raising program on already limited budgets?

Most libraries have Friends, and if your Friends group has many retirees, you have a good source of planned-giving prospects. Many libraries also have Friends who are volunteers—also a good source for prospects, leads, and helping hands to get a program started. The research capabilities of any library and librarian cannot be undervalued for a planned-giving program. Librarians may not have the answers, but they usually know where to look to find the answers. This skill is greatly beneficial to a good planned-giving program. Small budgets need not be a deterrent. Planned-giving programs need not be glitzy and expensive. Even a small bequest program can reap great benefits for the future.

Librarians are all familiar with the financial realities of providing services and materials on inadequate budgets. How realistic is it to consider another program when resources are already so stretched? The maxim "it takes money to make money" is true, and it would be unrealistic and foolish to think that a planned-giving program without designated funding can work. It is important for librarians and their boards to consider the importance of the long-range financial impact of a planned-giving program and to make a commitment of some level of support. Librarians and boards should be clear that planned giving is not the solution to short term and immediate financial problems, and that other fund-raising techniques and programs should be considered for those concerns. Planned giving is for future and long-term funding. In any event, without board support, the program will not prosper.

Elements of a Low-Cost Program

The most important elements of a planned-giving program do not necessarily cost a lot. These elements include volunteers, consultants, and the dissemination of information. The information, whether in the form of brochures, newsletters, events, or seminars, has the greatest potential for costs, but there are creative ways to keep such costs down.

Consultants

Consultants are key. Planned giving requires a high degree of specialized and detailed knowledge of estate planning, tax planning, and financial planning. Even the librarian's forte of knowing where to look for information is not enough for a successful planned-giving program. Knowing whom to ask for help is even more crucial. The consultant must also have no conflict of interest and must have sensitivity to the culture of your donors and your library. Best of all, the consultant should identify with your mission and be able to convey that to your donors. It would be ideal of course, if your consultant worked pro bono on your behalf.

Dissemination of Information

Estimates are that 80 percent of planned gifts are in the form of bequests.[3] Simply providing information on how to make a bequest or the creation of a bequest society can be the sum total of your planned-giving program. It does not cost much, and it greatly expands the possibility of future gifts to your library.

Bequest programs can vary greatly in sophistication and cost. A blurb on all publications, newsletters, or bookmarks can convey the simple straightforward message that your library wishes to be considered in a donor's estate planning. This makes your donors aware that your library can benefit from bequests. Be sure to include your legal name and address; attorneys creating bequest provisions for the donors need this information.

Creating a bequest society is another option for a successful bequest program. Again, there are costs incurred for this as well, including recognition events and publications. However, these can vary in sophistication and scope, and volunteers can greatly enhance the success of this endeavor as well.

Advisors

Professional advisors are a necessary ingredient to a planned-giving program, whether it is a deluxe program or one based on a shoestring budget. It is important for professional advisors to know of your program. Professional advisors include estate planning attorneys, accountants, and other financial planning professionals. These professional advisors can effectively facilitate the charitable gift—they can "make it happen." They can also be helpful as advisors to your library's planned-giving program.

Again, consider the Friends and volunteers who already support your library. Are there professionals among them who would consider serving on an advisory board? If you come up short in candidates for these advisory professionals, you might ask your Friends and volunteers if they would be willing to ask their own financial and estate planning professionals to help advise the library. Solicitations are uniquely successful when friends ask friends.

It might also be helpful to attend some programs sponsored by your area's planned-giving council to introduce yourself and delicately promote your library's planned-giving program. Interested professionals may well identify themselves to you through this effort of promotion. Planned-gift councils are comprised of attorneys, life insurance professionals, and accountants, as well as planned-giving officers from other institutions. Some areas have estate-planning councils whose membership includes attorneys, life insurance professionals, trust officers, and accountants, but not usually planned-giving officers from other institutions.

Leave a Legacy Campaigns

More and more communities are establishing a Leave a Legacy campaign, a community-based effort that encourages people from all walks of life to make gifts from their estates to the nonprofit organizations of their choice. The Leave a Legacy program is sponsored by the National Committee on Planned Giving (NCPG) and is based on a successful program started by the Central Ohio Planned Giving Council.

The Leave a Legacy program is a collaborative effort that includes community foundations, planned-giving professionals, and the media to educate the public about the benefits of leaving a legacy to the community. The Leave a Legacy program can provide speakers on planned giving to talk to your board and donors regarding planning giving. Community nonprofits can use the Leave a Legacy materials to send to their own donors and prospects.

If your community has a Leave a Legacy campaign program, you should definitely get your library involved in the program. It is an extremely effective method of beginning a planned-giving effort on a small budget. You can check with NCPG to see if your community has a program either by calling or by checking its Web site at http://www.ncpg.org/legacy.html

Volunteers

The dissemination of information in the form of brochures, newsletters, and events is another key element for a successful program, but it also represents an area of potential great cost. Are there printers among your Friends and volunteer organizations who might be willing to donate printing costs or to give your library a discount price for printing? Are there graphic designers who might donate their expertise in designing brochures or newsletters? You might also consider collaborating with other institutions, specifically other libraries in your area, on a campaign about the benefits of planned giving for the libraries in your community. Costs can be shared for printing and events. You might reach out to media professionals, including local newspaper and television stations, to publicize your library's new planned-giving program. A volunteer public relations professional can be of tremendous service.

There are many possibilities for creating a planned-giving program using assets you already have in the form of patrons, Friends, and volunteers. In fact, your Friends and volunteers are crucial to the success of your program for identifying prospects, helping solicit gifts, providing needed services, promoting your program, and sharing the vision of the library's future with the community at large. Your Friends and volunteers may well become your greatest benefactors . . . but only if you ask.

Notes

1. Jerold Panas, *Fund Raising Management* 25, no. 2 (April 1994): 4.
2. James E. Connell, "Communicating Charitable Estate Planning to Older Adults," *AHP Journal* (spring 1997): 29–32.
3. Robert R. Peters Jr., "Ten Key Strategies to Securing a Bequest," *Fund Raising Management* 26 (Feb. 1996): 44–47.

2

Building Blocks
of Planned Giving

The beginning point for planned giving is always the donor's philanthropic intent. Study after study has shown that people make charitable gifts because they believe in the work of the institution and want to further it. While legal and tax considerations can be very important, the person making the gift should always, first and foremost, believe in your library's mission. That said, it is often possible for a donor to make a substantial gift *and* save a significant amount of taxes. Because of the tax savings, the library can often receive an economic benefit far greater than the donor anticipated.

In order to facilitate a planned gift, it is very helpful for librarians to have some familiarity with the basic concepts of financial, tax, and estate planning. Although these are areas of professional specialization in their own right, it is important to be literate in them.

Financial planning involves identifying short-term (e.g., a down payment), mid-term (e.g., paying tuition), and long-term (e.g., funding retirement) financial goals and developing strategies to meet them. Tax planning focuses on minimizing the loss of accumulated wealth to taxes. Finally, estate planning is the planning necessary to accomplish two goals: to manage the estate during a person's lifetime; and to make arrangements for the timely and cost-effective distribution of assets upon the death of an individual and/or spouse, if any. Planned-giving vehicles are among the estate-planning tools that can allow individuals to meet these objectives.

Professional advisors (attorneys, certified public accountants, financial planners, insurance agents, and others) can be helpful on many levels. Not only are they professionals in their respective areas of expertise, but they have developed a relationship of trust with their clients (your prospects and/or donors) and frequently discuss deeply personal subjects with them, such as financial and family matters. As in all areas of planned giving, it is crucial to include allied professionals in your planned-giving program in as many ways as possible such as board and committee assignments and educational materials and programs.

Financial Planning

It is important to have some sense of your prospect's financial goals. This will help you develop some insight into how planned giving might help the donor to achieve them. Planned giving can facilitate the accomplishment of some financial goals by providing safe and secure yields, sometimes surpassing the yields on certificates of deposit, money market accounts, and certainly many stock dividends. Planned giving can also help the donor reduce or eliminate income taxes (including capital gains taxes), gift taxes, and estate taxes.

Information to Elicit

Keep your eyes and ears open for the following clues: Are there

>savings goals?
>assets needed for retirement?
>college costs ahead for children or grandchildren?
>nest-egg considerations?
>needs for a fixed and secure income stream?
>goals for increasing return on current investments?
>goals for reducing income taxes?
>capital gains considerations?
>goals for reducing estate and gift taxes?

Personal Financial Information

The most difficult adjustment for librarians is not the learning of the basics of financial planning, but rather the frightening idea of discussing these highly personal matters with prospects. Frequently, prospects will share such information quite openly because they understand it is important in order to facilitate their philanthropic and financial goals. Some prospects will share the information only if it is actively elicited. Some will choose to discuss these matters only with their professional advisors.

An attorney, CPA, and financial planning professionals can be very helpful members of the team in gathering or sharing financial information regarding a particular prospect or donor (with appropriate consent, of course). Typically they have questionnaires that go into great detail concerning a client's overall financial profile.

If you are comfortable asking a donor about personal financial information, the relevant information you need includes both personal and financial information.

Personal information such as:

Date of birth and social security number

Are there children? If so, what are their ages?

Are there grandchildren? If so, what are their ages?

Information on the spouse. Is he/she a U.S. citizen? (important for tax reasons)

Occupation

Income

Is there a will?

Is there a revocable living trust?

Are there any special needs such as handicapped children, college tuition concerns, elder care for parents?

Do they have professional advisors (financial, tax, and/or estate planning)? If so, who? (Prospects and donors are often reluctant to share this information.)

Financial information such as:

Investments	$_____
Cash	$_____
Equities	$_____
Fixed income	$_____

Mutual funds $_____

IRA/retirement $_____

Life insurance and/or cash
    surrender value $_____

Other $_____

Total assets to invest $_____

What types of assets?

Tax implications of assets?

Investment objectives (capital appreciation, capital appreciation
    plus income, income, capital preservation, reduced risk)

Retirement accounts

About liabilities

Is there debt?

Is the debt tax deductible?

A financial planner will also want to delve into the nature of his or her client's business holdings. If there is a closely held business, the financial planner will want to know the legal form of the business, whether it is incorporated or unincorporated, and, if incorporated, the form of the corporation (there are C corporations and S corporations, among others).

Although this can get complicated, it is important to keep in mind that a charitable remainder trust cannot be a holder of S corporation stock, though a donor can make an outright gift of S corporation stock to your library. The library will likely be subject to some income tax, however. If this issue of S corporation stock comes up in a discussion with a donor, it is time to seek the advice of an attorney or CPA. For a more thorough discussion of this issue, see chapter 3.

Other relevant information about the closely held business includes whether there are other owners involved; whether the business is capital intensive or a personal service company; whether other family members are working in the business; whether there is a succession plan (transfer of leadership of the business in the event of retirement, disability, or death); and, how much of the donor's estate is represented by the business.

Again, as a librarian, you might not feel entirely comfortable going into great depth about the donor's business. However, in cultivating the personal relationship with the donor, it will be helpful to get an overall sense of the donor's business. How does the donor feel about the business? What about the future prospects for the business? What will happen to the business when the donor retires? Are there family members involved in the business? Is there a succession plan?

There are some common problems for business owners you should keep in mind. Is the donor the source of value for the business? If the owner were to retire, become disabled, or die, would the business lose some or all of its value? Is the donor's sense of self-worth tied partially or completely to the business? Is the donor realistic about the true value of the business?

The Portfolio Mix

A portfolio may contain bonds, preferred stocks, and common stocks of various types of enterprises. You will find that many prospects, especially those who felt the impact of the Great Depression, are heavily invested in liquid fixed income investments, including

Savings accounts. These deposit accounts are generally insured by the federal government up to $100,000. The money can be withdrawn whenever the depositor chooses. While there is a guaranteed return, there is no opportunity for appreciation of capital nor protection against inflation. Rates typically rise and fall with inflation and recession.

Certificates of deposit (CDs). Like other deposit accounts, CDs are generally insured up to $100,000. A CD is a receipt for funds deposited with a financial institution payable to the holder at some specified date and bearing interest at a fixed rate. There are generally penalties for withdrawing the money early.

Money market funds. These have replaced savings accounts as the basic savings vehicle for many families. Their yields are often higher than those of savings accounts, three-month CDs, and some longer-term CDs. Like other mutual funds, money market funds pool your money with the money of other investors to buy a portfolio of securities such as "IOUs" issued by companies; U.S. Treasury bills; and other short-term, generally low-risk investments. Money market funds are not federally insured, and yields go up and down with prevailing interest rates. These funds usually come with check writing privileges of $500 or more.

Short-term bond funds. Short-term bonds pose some additional risk compared to money market funds, but their yields are sometimes higher by as much as one or two percentage points. These funds, in essence, lend money to corporations and other borrowers. The price of shares in short-term bond funds fluctuates with interest rates. The price goes up when interest rates fall, and the price goes down when interest rates rise.

The investments discussed so far are relatively low on the risk scale, and they offer a steady stream of income. Because the rates of return on these investments are so low, some planned-giving vehicles, such as charitable gift annuities and pooled income funds, might offer the charitably inclined individual higher rates of return and therefore greater income. These planned-giving options are very attractive to donors in their seventies and eighties who have traditionally invested in very conservative portfolios.

Bonds

Bonds are another investment option. A bond is simply evidence of a debt. Essentially, bonds represent long-term IOUs. Governments, agencies of the U.S. government, or corporations can issue them. Cities and states also issue bonds. (They are called municipal bonds, or "munis.") When you buy a bond you are, in effect, financing a loan to the bond issuer. Investors literally become creditors of the entity issuing the bond.

As with other loans, the borrower pays interest to the lender. Unlike stock dividends, which change along with company profit levels, the interest payments on a bond are usually fixed. This steady income is the main reason that some investors are attracted to bonds. This income will come to sudden halt, of course, if the borrower defaults. When the bond matures, the bondholders are repaid their principal in full. As noted above, bond prices increase when interest rates fall and decrease when interest rates rise.

Different types of bonds carry different levels of risk. Government bonds are generally considered to be safer investments, while corporate bonds generally carry higher degrees of risk.

Forms of Bonds

Following is a description of some of the forms of bonds you will likely encounter, and some of their attributes.

A *municipal bond* is issued by a state or a political subdivision such as a county, city, town, or village. The term also designates bonds issued by state agencies and authorities. In general, interest paid on municipal bonds is exempt from federal income taxes and from state and local income taxes within the state of issue. Since municipals are tax free, they are generally offered at a lower rate of interest than most corporate bonds. But for someone in the 39.6 percent tax bracket, a tax-free bond yielding 6 percent gives this individual a return equivalent to a taxable interest of 9.9 percent. Not bad. Note that the safety of municipal bonds correlates directly to the creditworthiness of the issuer. Recently even some of the largest municipalities have had trouble redeeming bonds that they have issued.

U.S. government securities can provide interest, income, and staggered maturities such as two, five, ten, and thirty years. The interest is not subject to state and local taxes. If held to maturity, the investor will receive the principal and promised interest payments. Note, however, that if interest rates rise, the sales price will drop. So being able to hold the security until maturity becomes an important planning consideration. These securities come in three varieties: Treasury bills, Treasury notes, and Treasury bonds.

> *Treasury bills* are short-term government paper with no stated interest rate. They are sold at a discount in competitive bidding and reach maturity in ninety days or less. Yields usually beat the average yields on bank CDs of the same length of maturity, and they sometimes yield more than money market funds. Additionally, income from "T-bills" is not subject to state and local taxes. The minimum investment is $10,000. Note that rising interest rates can cause the selling price of government securities to drop. So these shares are most attractive when interest rates are stable or falling.

> *Treasury notes* are U.S. government paper, not legally restricted as to interest rates, with maturities from one to five years.

> *Treasury bonds* are U.S. government bonds issued in $1,000 units with maturity dates of five years or longer. They are traded on the open market like other bonds.

U.S. savings bonds, Series E and EE, offer a very high level of security. Redemption values typically rise every six months, in line with prevailing interest rates. Purchasers of EE bonds are guaranteed a minimum return of slightly over 4 percent if they hold a bond for 17 years. These bonds offer a special tax advantage. The owner may report the income on his or her tax return as it accrues or in a lump sum when the bonds are redeemed (when the owner may be retired and in a lower income tax bracket). Additionally, if they are redeemed for qualified educational expenses (tuition and fees) for the investor, spouse, or dependents, there is no tax if redemption occurs in the year the expense is incurred. The minimum investment is $25 for a $50 savings bond that can be redeemed for $50 in 17 years or less.

Series H and HH bonds do not have the special tax advantage that E and EE bonds have. Interest is paid semiannually and must be reported each year. These bonds mature ten years after they are issued. They can be redeemed any time after six months from the date of issue.

Corporate bonds are evidence of indebtedness issued by a corporation, rather than by the U.S. government or a municipality. The bond can be secured (backed by a mortgage or lien on specific property) or it may be unsecured, a debenture bond (backed by the general credit of the company). Obviously, secured bonds are a safer investment. Disadvantages of corporate bonds are that interest is fixed, so market value will decline in inflationary periods. Additionally, interest on bonds (except municipals) is taxable income. Finally, the ultimate safety of corporate bonds is dependent on the financial health of the issuer and the company's continuing ability to pay interest and repay principal.

Convertible bonds may be exchanged by the owner for common stock or other securities, usually of the same company, in accordance with the terms of the issue. These bonds, then, offer the security of a fixed return investment and the growth opportunities of an equity (stock) investment.

EXAMPLE _____

By now you might be wondering, "Why the inverse relationship between interest rates and bond prices?" Consider the following example: Mr. Donor purchases a 30-year Treasury bond for $1,000 at par (which means the price equals the face value on the bond). The coupon payments are $100 per year, so the interest rate that Mr. Donor is getting is 10 percent. He will always get a 10 percent yield if he holds the bond until maturity at 30 years regardless of what the market interest rates do. Whether interest rates rise or fall in the market, they will not affect the yield that Mr. Donor receives on the bond.

Assume that interest rates rise to 12 percent, and Mr. Donor wants to take advantage of the higher rates by selling his bond and reinvesting in a new bond that pays a coupon of $120 per year (12 percent interest). He will not be able to sell the bond for what he paid for it ($1,000). Why? Because nobody would pay for a 10 percent interest rate what he paid for it ($1,000) when the going market rate is 12 percent. Consequently, Mr. Donor will have to sell the bond at a discount, something less than $1,000, so that when the bond reaches maturity in 30 years, and the buyer cashes it in for $1,000, it will be equivalent to getting a 12 percent rate of return. The new buyer of the bond will still only get the $100 coupons on the original bond, but he will also get $1,000 at the end of the 30 years even though he paid less than that, say $800.

This explains why bond prices in the market fall when current interest rates rise. They fall because the next buyer of the bond will have to get a discount on the bond's value so that it will yield the higher current market rate.

Stocks and Mutual Funds

Stock shares represent ownership in a corporation. When an individual buys stock in a corporation, he or she becomes a part owner or shareholder. Investors generally profit when the company profits (and vice versa!). They also have a say in some of the company's major decisions. As a general rule, the better the economy, the more money a company's investors make (by way of both dividends and capital appreciation).

Historically, stocks have been the best option for those seeking long-run, inflation-beating returns. Stocks have historically outpaced inflation by 7 percent per year. The analogous figure for bonds is only 2 percent. Treasury bills have outpaced inflation by merely one half of one percentage point. Inflation has averaged 3.1 percent over the past seventy years. Stocks usually make money for investors as long as they are held for five years and as long as the portfolio is well diversified.

Investors can earn money either from stock dividends (payments made to stockholders by some corporations) or from selling the stock at a price higher than they paid for it. The latter is called capital appreciation; the profit realized from capital appreciation is called a capital gain. If the investor loses money, it is called a capital loss. The difference between the cost basis (usually the purchase price) and its fair market value on the date of sale (the current price) is capital gain and is subject to income taxation. Typically, capital gain income is taxed at a lower rate than ordinary income. Donors can make a gift of appreciated stock and receive a charitable income tax deduction for the full fair market value of the stock and also avoid capital gains taxation. This is why it is cheaper to give away appreciated property (including stock) rather than cash.

Two very important types of stocks often held by prospects are blue chip stocks and growth stocks. Blue chip stocks are shares of companies known nationally for the quality and wide acceptance of their products or services, and for their ability to make money and pay dividends. Examples include AT&T, IBM, Xerox, and Disney. These stocks usually pay dividends that, even though they are considered to be low yielding (2 percent to 4 percent), are considered to be relatively safe and dependable. Gift annuities and pooled income funds (discussed in chapter 3) can usually increase considerably the income stream to charitably minded individuals over blue chip stock dividends.

Growth stocks represent shares of companies with a record of relatively rapid growth earnings. Growth stocks usually pay low or no dividends but provide far greater opportunity for growth (capital appreciation) over time. In recent years, we have seen phenomenal growth in start-up companies in the high technology fields that has turned many people into multimillionaires. Growth stocks provide greater opportunities for making money but also carry much higher risk for investors because of market volatility. Charitable remainder trusts are often used by charitably inclined individuals so that appreciated growth stock can be sold without having to pay income taxes on the capital appreciation.

A mutual fund is an "open-end" investment company that continually offers new shares to the public in addition to redeeming shares on demand as required by law. In other words, a mutual fund is a collection of stocks, bonds, or other securities purchased and managed by an investment company with the capital from a group of investors. Money is pooled with that of other investors. The investment company then invests this collective pool in a variety of stocks, bonds, or other securities.

Some mutual funds pay dividends based on the underlying dividends offered by the stocks and the interest payments offered the bonds in the fund.

Some mutual funds hold securities that offer the potential for capital appreciation. When these securities are sold by the fund, the fund distributes the profits from the sale to its investors. Mutual funds distribute these earnings annually in the form of capital gains. The investment return and principal value of mutual funds will fluctuate so that an investor's shares, when redeemed, may be worth more or less than their original cost.

Many mutual funds attempt to accomplish specific investment objectives, such as current income, long-term growth, and preservation of capital. Specific examples include money market funds, tax-free money market funds, municipal bond funds, income funds, balanced funds, growth and income funds, growth funds, international and global funds, sector funds (such as electronics, energy, or health care), and aggressive growth funds (which aim for maximum capital appreciation and typically invest in the stock of emerging or out-of-favor companies). Among the primary advantages of mutual funds are diversification of investments and professional management. As with stocks, mutual fund shares (especially those that have appreciated significantly in value) can be donated to your library and the donor will receive full fair market value and an income tax charitable deduction. The donor will also avoid taxation of any capital gain.

Diversification is how sophisticated investors reduce risk—by spreading their dollars across a variety of investments to protect against poor performance by any single investment. By combining different types of investments, investors can design a portfolio that is more consistent with their desired combination of risk tolerance and return than any single investment could provide. Additionally, because each type of investment performs differently under different market conditions, their performance together tends to balance over time, helping to stabilize the value of the portfolio as a whole.

Asset allocation refers to how an investor's money is divided among various types of investments. For example, an investor might decide to put 50 percent of her assets in stocks, 30 percent in bonds and 20 percent in a money market fund. Asset classes include

cash (e.g., cash and cash equivalents like money market funds and CDs)

fixed principal (e.g., fixed annuities and trust deeds)

debt (e.g., government and corporate bonds)

equity (e.g., stocks, interests in closely held businesses and mutual funds)

tangibles (e.g., real estate, art, precious metals, and other valuable collectibles)

It might surprise you to learn that 91 percent of a portfolio's overall return comes from asset allocation (between stocks and bonds). Only 6 percent is derived from the specific investment selections. Three percent of the return is accounted for by other variables.

Here are some examples:

During the twenty-year period between 1977 and 1996, a portfolio invested 100 percent in equities (an unmanaged index of 500 widely held stocks) has had an average annual return of 15.3 percent.

During the twenty-year period between 1977 and 1996, a portfolio invested 60 percent in equities and 40 percent in debt (intermediate term government bonds) has had an average annual return of 13 percent.

During the twenty-year period between 1977 and 1996, a portfolio invested 50 percent in equities and 50 percent in debt has had an average annual return of 12.4 percent.

During the twenty-year period between 1977 and 1996, a portfolio invested 100 percent in debt has had an average annual return of 9.4 percent.

As you can see, the greater the risk (the percentage of equities), the greater the reward. In order to round out the financial planning perspective, following is a list of types of investment ranked according to the level of inherent risk (those listed at the top carry the lowest risk and those listed at the bottom carry the highest):

Money market mutual funds, cash, savings accounts, and certificates of deposits, life insurance cash values

Fixed annuities, municipal bond mutual funds

Your home, balanced mutual funds

Common stocks, growth mutual funds

Oil and gas interests, raw land

Commodities

Real Estate

Portfolios often include real estate. A residence can be the largest asset owned by the prospective donor. Other real estate may include commercial property, residential rental property, vacant land, and vacation homes. Gifts of real estate involve many factors, which will be discussed later.

Life Insurance

Life insurance can serve any number of purposes, and the number of life insurance products on the market is mind boggling. Let's focus on a few highlights. Life insurance:

Can be a source of tax-sheltered money for capital accumulation

Can be a source of money that immediately mushrooms in value upon the death of the insured. Can be used to pay the deceased's debts, e.g., the mortgage, funeral expenses, and income or estate taxes. The possibilities are numerous. Additionally, the proceeds can usually be transferred expeditiously because they avoid the probate process.

Offers the creation of an estate immediately

Can pay for itself in the event of disability

Builds up a cash value that can be borrowed against (a forced savings device)

May finance retirement through a tax-free policy loan

Can be converted at retirement to a favorable annuity program

Can pass to heirs as income and is often estate-tax free

Is exempt from estate tax when the insurance policy is legally owned by someone other than the insured; e.g., the policy is owned by an irrevocable life insurance trust.

TYPES OF LIFE INSURANCE

The "lingo" is complex and often confusing, so there is no substitute for real due diligence before purchasing an insurance policy. For estate planning purposes, there are two primary types of insurance, term and permanent. Term insurance provides a preset amount of cash if the insured dies within a set period of time. Term insurance is the least expensive form of coverage for the short term. Permanent insurance is the only coverage guaranteed for life. The company can never cancel the policy so long as premiums are paid. It is automatically renewable without a new physical examination of the insured. Over time, permanent insurance builds up a cash value, which produces returns for the policyholder. These returns accumulate tax free.

Permanent insurance comes in three flavors—whole life, universal life, and variable life. Whole life insurance provides a set dollar amount of coverage and is guaranteed for life in exchange for fixed, uniform payments. Universal life is term insurance combined with an investment account or side fund. It is not necessarily guaranteed for life. The policyholder builds up a cash reserve but can also vary premium payments, amount of coverage, or both, from year to year. Variable life insurance refers to both whole life and universal life where the cash reserves are invested in securities, stocks, and bonds. This is great when the market is going up but provides unpleasant surprises when the financial markets decline.

Survivorship life insurance, or "second-to-die" or "joint" life insurance, provides a single policy that insures two lives, usually spouses. The policy only pays off on the death of the second (surviving) spouse. This form of insurance is designed mainly for use as part of an estate plan for high-net-worth couples who expect to owe substantial estate taxes on the death of the second (surviving) spouse. Because two lives are insured, premiums for these policies are low as compared to policies on one person's life.

Information on the donor's financial situation will help focus on the financial planning aspect of charitable gift planning. An attorney, CPA, or professional financial advisor can help immeasurably in sharing relevant financial information and providing a financial snapshot of your donor's needs. However, not all donors have financial advisors. (You might suggest a few.) Getting as much information as possible will enable you to offer planned-giving opportunities that match the prospect's objectives and style. It is important to consider the makeup of the donor's investment portfolio, not only for its assets, but also for the style of investing. This can help you to determine the type of planned-giving structure that will best meet your donor's needs.

Tax Planning

Although there are many tax-based incentives for making charitable gifts, charitable intent—and not tax savings—should always be the primary motivating factor. Why? Because in even the best of charitable gift plans, the donor "gives up" something—that's why it's called a gift. There is usually a financial cost, and that is why the donor gets an income, gift, or estate-tax charitable deduction.

For example, if a donor purchases a charitable gift annuity and retains an income interest, the donor has still given away the principal, permanently. Tax savings are a reward from the federal government because it wants to encourage charitable giving as a matter of public policy. Charitable gift planning can have an impact on three different taxes—income taxes, including capital gains taxes; gift taxes; and estate taxes.

As a general rule, people do not enjoy making charitable gifts to the Internal Revenue Service! (Though we have met some people who do not mind paying transfer taxes.) Therefore, much of tax planning and charitable gift planning involves preventing the unnecessary waste of estate assets through the payment of taxes. The result of this process is to maximize the net income that the donor's beneficiaries (including the library) will receive after the payment of all taxes. This chapter explores the taxation of investments, the basic structure of the transfer tax (gift and estate), and what is included in the estate.

Taxation plays a very important role in the estate planning and financial planning process. The income received from dividends, interest, rents, and so on is taxed at the regular income tax rates of 15, 28, 31, 36 and 39.6 percent. Profits or losses resulting from a sale of property or securities also have tax implications (capital gains and capital losses, respectively).

Adjusted Basis

When one sells a capital asset, an income tax is owed on the difference between the sale price and what is called the "adjusted basis" of the asset. If the sale price is less than the adjusted basis, then it results in a tax loss; if it is more, a gain.

Generally, the adjusted basis is the original purchase price of the asset plus any related additional capital expenditures. For example, if one paid $30,000 for property and made $10,000 of capital improvements over the years, the adjusted basis is $40,000. There are numerous exceptions to the general rule. For example, for inherited property, the estate tax valuation establishes its basis. The property in a decedent's estate is generally valued at its fair market value on the date of death. The result is that the property receives a new basis that may be higher or lower than the decedent's. If lower, this "paper loss" is never realized. If higher, the unrealized appreciation escapes capital gains taxation.

EXAMPLE _____

Mrs. Anderson invested in securities in the late 1940s at $50 per share. When she dies, the stock is being traded at $100 per share. Her son, who inherits her estate, gets a new basis of $100. If he sells it for $107, the taxable gain is only $7 versus $57 if the $50 purchase price were used as the basis.

The Taxpayer Relief Act of 1997 lowered capital gains taxes starting July 29, 1997, to the following levels:

20 percent for holding periods of twelve months or more before sale

28 percent for collectibles (art, coins, etc.)

25 percent for depreciation recapture on real estate

The most typical scenario with prospective donors is a contemplated gift of low basis, highly appreciated stock that has been held for many, many years. The 20 percent capital gains tax would apply to a sale under this scenario.

A basic understanding of the gift and estate tax system is important. This is well within the domain of professional advisors, but some understanding of the basic terminology and concepts is imperative. These taxes are imposed on an individual's transfer of property to someone else and are often called transfer taxes. Transfer tax rates range from 37 percent to 55 percent, and the rate brackets rise to the 55 percent level very quickly.

"Estate tax" is a friendly way of saying "death tax." This is a tax on the transfer of property at death. All of the property one owns is subject to federal estate taxes. The good news, however, is that most estates are not large enough to be taxed. Why? Because no estate taxes are due if the net value of the taxable estate transferred at one's death is less than $675,000 to $1,000,000, depending on the date of death.

Estate tax rates are very high, ranging from 37 percent to 55 percent for estates over $3,000,000. Additionally, several states (though not most) impose their own death taxes on property of a deceased who lived or owned real estate in that state.

Estate Tax Exemptions. A combination of federal tax law exemptions and deductions makes it possible to leave substantial amounts of wealth free of transfer taxes. Among them is the transfer tax exclusion. This allows a set dollar amount of property to pass tax-free, no matter to whom it is left. Each individual can shelter $675,000 of lifetime or death-time transfers from taxes in 2000. A tax credit reduces taxes dollar-for-dollar. The transfer tax exclusion is a use-it-or-lose-it benefit. If a person's gift and estate taxes are not sufficient to absorb the credit, then the credit is lost. Consequently, the most basic concept of estate planning for a married couple is not to waste the unified credit of the first spouse to die. See table 2.1.

Table 2.1 Amount You Can Transfer without Paying Tax

Year of Death	Transfer Tax Exclusion
2000	$ 675,000
2001	$ 675,000
2002	$ 700,000
2003	$ 700,000
2004	$ 850,000
2005	$ 950,000
2006 and after	$1,000,000

Note that the major increases occur in the later years, so these increases do not provide a lot of safety from a planning point of view. In essence, the increase amounts to no more than an inflation adjustment. A prospect's asset base may well grow at a faster pace. One should not be lulled into a false sense of security.

If $650,000 or $1 million sounds like a lot to you, then consider the following. Here is a checklist of what might be included in your estate: real estate, securities (stocks, bonds, and mutual funds), interest and dividends that you are owed that have not been paid, bank accounts, all tangible personal property, the full face value of life insurance policies that you own, no-fault insurance payments due to you, annuities paid by contract or agreement, value of any qualified retirement plan including IRAs, claims paid for pain and suffering even after your death (but not claims for wrongful death), income tax refunds, forgiven debts, dower and courtesy rights, Uniform Gifts to Minors Act and Uniform Transfer to Minors Act custodial accounts for which you are the custodian if you created the accounts and closely held businesses. As you can see, the value of your estate may well be much greater than you thought.

If the decedent made taxable gifts during his or her lifetime, then the amount of the personal exemption is reduced. Currently, an individual can give away as much as $10,000 to each of any number of recipients without paying gift taxes on the transfers. If a married individual's spouse agrees to "split" a gift, as much as $20,000 may be given to each recipient annually even if the money comes from only one spouse.

This so-called gift-tax annual exclusion is a big tax break. By making annual gifts that qualify for the exclusion, a person can reduce his or her estate significantly in a fairly short amount of time. These gifts are not tax deductible, but you pay no tax when the gift is made and neither does the recipient.

Additionally, no gift tax is imposed on payments made on behalf of anyone for tuition or medical care so long as the payments are made directly to an educational institution or provider of medical services.

As of 1981, transfers between husband and wife are 100 percent transfer-tax-free at death.

Last, and by no means least is the estate tax charitable deduction, which exempts all property left to a nonprofit, such as the library. All gifts made to nonprofits are exempt from federal gift and estate taxes. Like the marital deduction, the charitable deduction is unlimited. So, there is no estate tax if your prospect gives his or her entire estate to the library! And, unlike the income tax law, there are no percentage limitations or ceilings.

If an estate is likely to be subject to estate taxation, then several questions need to be asked and answered so that appropriate steps can be taken and appropriate plans put into effect. For example, how can one eliminate or reduce estate taxes while achieving other estate planning goals at the same time? Where will the money come from to pay the estate taxes? Now we are squarely within the realm of estate planning.

Estate Planning

Some people work incredibly hard to create and accumulate wealth, yet for some inexplicable reason they do nothing to preserve it. Estate planning, however, is not simply about preserving wealth. Estate planning can tighten or tear the family structure. Obviously, the stakes are high, and these matters should rest ultimately in the hands of competent professionals.

Over the years, we have seen a number of definitions of estate planning:

> The creation, conservation, and utilization of family resources to obtain the maximum support and security for the family during the lifetime and after the death of the planner.

> The art of continuing to prosper when you are alive, then dying with the smallest taxable estate and probate estate possible and passing your property to your loved ones with a minimum of fuss and expense.

Both of these definitions allude to the passing of wealth from one generation to the next. This is serious complex business because it involves human motives and values and should not be taken lightly because the stakes are so high. Typically, one part of every estate plan is a will. Everyone needs a will, not just the "rich." So let's talk about wills for a moment.

Since a vast majority of Americans do not have a will, let's start off with a simple definition: A will is a legal document that specifies how assets are to be distributed at your death and names guardians for minor children, if any. If you die without a will ("intestate"), you will have lost control over what happens to your property and who will care for your minor children, if you have any. For example, your estate might pass to a former husband's second wife rather than to your children of his first marriage! Children are typically treated equally. Real world experience shows that this is often not what parents want. Do you want to choose your beneficiaries, or let the law do so?

Any property transferred by will is subject to probate. Probate is the legal process of proving, or verifying, your will through the courts. Because the process can be slow and costly, probate has a bad reputation. This is why, in recent years, so many people have opted for a living trust to transfer most of their property outside the probate process.

In addition, in some states, probate fees are based on the gross value of the estate. This means that the liabilities are net income when determining the cost of probate. As a result, trusts may be more favorable because they avoid the high cost of probate fees in certain states.

A will can be changed as often as one wishes (a point that your library should keep in mind during the donor stewardship process).

As with a will, a trust is a written document that transfers property. But while a will is a statement of what the donor wants to happen to his or her possessions after death, a trust is a multipurpose tool that individuals can use to

> manage property
>
> distribute assets to beneficiaries
>
> avoid probate, which can be a very lengthy and costly process
>
> save on taxes (in the case of irrevocable trusts)
>
> protect privacy
>
> provide for disability
>
> avoid potentially contentious, costly, and drawn out court proceedings.

Strategies to Reduce the Federal Estate Tax

Based on our discussion of the structure and operation of the federal gift and estate tax system, here are some basic tax reduction approaches.

Be generous. Make the tax-exempt gifts of $10,000 to $20,000 if you can afford to do so. This is actually the most effective way to reduce one's gross estate. And in addition to removing the principal from the trust, significant amounts of subsequent appreciation can be removed as well. Note that the annual gift exclusion ($10,000) does not reduce the transfer tax exclusion ($675,000 in 2000).

Create the right kind of trust. The most typical form of trust is a form of "bypass trust" called an AB trust (also called a "marital life estate trust," a "credit shelter trust," or an "exemption trust.")

Trusts

The bypass trust is a revocable living trust that can offer substantial savings in federal estate taxes. Each person has a federal estate and gift transfer tax exclusion of $675,000 in 2000 that is scheduled to increase in annual increments up to $1 million in 2006. The federal estate tax after the application of the $675,000 exclusion starts at the rate of 37 percent and graduates quite rapidly up to 55 percent on the portion of the estate in excess of $3 million. If a person leaves property to his or her spouse upon death, there is no estate tax. (Spouses can give unlimited amounts to each other free from any transfer taxes.) However, such property will be included in the estate of the surviving spouse upon that person's subsequent death. Therefore, if a couple has an estate of $1,300,000 and on the death of one spouse all of the property is left outright to the surviving spouse, upon the death of the surviving spouse there would be an estate tax on the portion of the estate in excess of the surviving spouse's transfer tax exclusion of $675,000.

Alternatively, suppose the couple establishes a living trust and $675,000 is placed in a special "by-pass" subtrust to be activated upon the death of either spouse. Upon the death of the surviving spouse, the $675,000 in the by-pass subtrust would not be included in that person's estate. This would result in very substantial estate tax savings, with more property being passed to the couple's children or other heirs (or the library!). Why? Because the surviving spouse never legally owned the trust property. The surviving spouse may nevertheless receive all of the income, can draw on the principal of the by-pass subtrust with certain limited restrictions, and can be the trustee (the person who manages the trust, makes investment decisions, and so on) of the entire trust, including the by-pass subtrust. If the amount in the by-pass subtrust appreciates in value during the lifetime of the surviving spouse, then the appreciated amount will not be subject to estate taxes upon that person's death. This is a very attractive feature of trust planning, indeed.

When the surviving spouse dies, the trust property goes to the final beneficiaries specified in the trust document (oftentimes the children).

Here are brief descriptions of some fancy trusts.

QTIP trusts. A trust that allows a married person to name the surviving spouse as the life beneficiary of the trust property. When the second spouse dies, the property passes to the final beneficiaries named by the first spouse.

Life insurance trust. A trust set up to buy life insurance coverage or to become the owner of an existing policy. When a policy is owned by a trust, the death benefit is not counted as part of the insured person's estate for estate-tax purposes.

Qualified personal residence trust. A complicated trust that can be used to remove your home or vacation home from your estate.

Charitable remainder trust. This trust lets people leave assets to a favored charity and receive a tax break but still retain income for life or for a term of years (not to exceed twenty). This works best for people with a valuable, highly appreciated asset that if sold would generate large capital-gains taxes.

Charitable lead trust. A trust that pays a charity income from a donated asset for a set number of years, after which time the principal goes to the donor's beneficiaries with reduced (sometimes to zero!) transfer taxes.

Generation-skipping trusts. This form of trust provides income to one generation of beneficiaries (called the middle or second generation) and then leaves the trust property outright to the next, or third, generation. Up to $1 million or $2 million for a couple, will avoid further estate tax when the second generation dies. The trust principal is left in trust for one's grandchildren, with one's children receiving only trust income. The generation-skipping tax is a flat 55 percent. This is a transfer tax assessed on gifts in excess of $1 million to grandchildren, great-grandchildren, or others at least two generations after the donor.

There are a number of strategies that can be used to accomplish philanthropic and financial objectives. Some of these techniques are planned-giving techniques, and some are not. Again, general estate planning is the stage on which the charitable gift planning acts. Donors naturally want to take care of their family and others first, and then the nonprofits that are meaningful to them. Almost everyone agrees that minimizing or eliminating the percentage of the estate that goes to the IRS is a good thing. Incidentally, the IRS is a bona fide nonprofit. But most contributions to this particular charity are involuntary.

Again, the purpose of this chapter is to expose you to some important terminology and broad concepts, and not to intimidate you. Leave the technical pieces to the specialists. They are good at it. Your job is to be an enthusiastic advocate for the mission of your library. Play your role as a member of the planned giving team well, and good things are bound to happen. We have seen it happen time and time again.

3

Boosting Philanthropy with Charitable Gift Planning

Tax rules governing charitable gifts and the tax benefits available to donors have become increasingly complex. Issues meriting serious consideration include, for example, the type of property to be contributed, such as cash, appreciated securities, real estate, or other kinds of non-cash assets. The manner in which the contribution is made should be fully evaluated. For example, an outright gift versus a life income gift or a bequest. Calculation of the proper charitable income, gift, or estate tax deduction involves several factors and requires careful attention.

The idea of helping to structure a donor's gift may well be daunting to a librarian. The various planned giving terms of art, e.g., charitable remainder trusts, charitable lead trusts, and deferred gift annuities, may cause some dread and confusion. Like having a basic knowledge of financial, tax, and estate planning, it is important for the librarian to have a basic understanding of the range of planned-giving options and a sense of which assets might work in a given plan. With more complex gifts, librarians should always recommend that the donor seek the advice of the appropriate professional advisor(s). So, too, should the library have professional specialists assist in structuring the more complex gifts on its behalf. Nevertheless, it is important to know enough to be able to recognize a planned-giving opportunity when it knocks on your library's door. See figure 3.1.

At the end of this chapter we look at some typical donor "profiles" and assess their needs and the types of charitable gift plans that often help them achieve their philanthropic and financial goals.

Clues That Can Help Match Potential Donors and Giving Opportunities
(If the prospect says this, then think "planned gift!")

1. "I'm planning to sell the house."
2. "My funds are all tied up in my company."
3. "I can't give to the library now because I'm saving for retirement."
4. "The kids are up and out, but how can I help my grandchildren with those college bills?"
5. "I'd like to help, but I want to leave my estate intact for my family."
6. "This place is really getting to be a burden, but if we sell it, the capital gains bite will be huge."
7. "I'm locked into stock I've had for years. It doesn't pay as much as I'd like, but I'd be hit with big capital gains taxes if I sold it."
8. "I can't give anything now because of my health problems, but I think that the library is doing wonderful things."

Figure 3.1   Door Openers to Planned Giving

When Is a Gift a Gift?

Lifetime charitable gifts are considered to be made on the date of delivery—that point when the donor no longer has dominion and control over the asset. Determining the date of delivery is important for several reasons: (a) it determines the tax year in which the gift may be deducted by the donor; (b) for assets that fluctuate in value, it is the date on which the gift is valued; and (c) it determines whether the gift is of long-term or short-term capital gain property. The rules can be complex. Here is a summary of some of the rules for very common charitable transfers.

Gifts by Check. A contribution made by check is deemed made in the year in which the check is delivered or mailed to the charity, even though the charity does not receive the check until the following year. The donor, however, cannot place conditions on the time or manner of payment, and the check must be honored when presented to the bank. If the check is not honored, for example, because of insufficient funds, then the gift will not be deemed to have been made in the year in which it was delivered or mailed.

Gifts of Stock. A gift of stock is deemed made when the donor delivers the stock certificate to the nonprofit, duly endorsed or with a signed stock power. If the securities are hand delivered to the nonprofit by the donor, then the delivery date is the day on which the nonprofit receives the securities. If the donor mails the securities to the nonprofit or to his or her broker or other agent, then the date of delivery is the date of mailing, provided that the securities are received in the "ordinary course of the mail."

If the donor delivers the stock to his or her bank or broker (acting as his or her agent) or to the issuing corporation (or its agent) with instructions to reissue the stock in the name of the charity, then the delivery date is the day on which the stock is transferred to the charity's name on the corporation's books. Because the donor loses control over the delivery date, the gift may not be deemed delivered until the next year, and the gift will be valued as of the date the corporation makes the change on its books.

Other examples of when a gift is a gift include:

A contribution charged to a credit card is deductible in the year the charge is made;

delivery of a donor's own promissory note is not deemed payment, and the deduction is deferred, until the note is actually paid, and

a gift of real estate is complete upon the execution and delivery of the deed to the nonprofit.

The Income Tax Charitable Deduction

Special Rules for Tangible Personal Property

A donor who owns valuable tangible personal property such as original works of art, an automobile, or household furnishings may contribute the property to the library. However, federal tax rules place restrictions on this kind of property in terms of the income tax charitable deduction available to the donor.

For a gift of tangible personal property related to the library's tax exempt function, the donor may take an income tax charitable deduction for the full fair market value of the property, as determined by a qualified appraisal. A gift of property with an unrelated use will provide the donor with a deduction limited to the cost basis of the property (generally the original purchase price). These rules do not apply to testamentary gifts, however, where a 100 percent estate tax charitable deduction is available, whether the use is related or unrelated.

Clearly, books donated to a library will pass the related use test. It is likely that works of art would also pass muster if the art is displayed, since it enhances the library's environment. A gift of livestock, however, would probably not pass the related use test and would be a better asset to donate to an agriculture department at a university or college.

No Deduction Allowed?

Some items of value are not deductible. The value of a donor's personal time or services and automobile depreciation, insurance, or general maintenance and repairs are not deductible. For example, consider the case of a photographer who publishes a book and wishes to donate that book to your library. The photographer can deduct only the costs of the supplies used to create the book, not the value of the time spent creating the photographs and the book itself. Authors and playwrights who donate their personal works of literature are limited to a charitable income tax deduction equal to the cost basis of their work; that is, what the supplies cost them to produce the work.

Substantiation and Disclosure

Donors must properly claim and substantiate charitable contributions to be entitled to the income, gift, or estate tax charitable deduction.

For a gift of cash, the receipt from the library need only show the name of the donee, the contribution date, and the amount of the contribution. A letter from the library is sufficient. For a gift of property, the receipt must show the name of the library, the date, the location of the contribution, and a description of the property in some detail. The value is not required in the receipt.

Donors making gifts of $250 or more may not rely on the substantiation methods described above (a simple letter or a canceled check will not suffice). Those donors must instead receive a contemporaneous, written acknowledgment from the library. Otherwise, the gift is not deductible. The receipt must be provided to the donor on or before the date that the donor's tax return is due, and it must include:

The amount of cash donated and a description, *but not the value*, of any property contributed.

A statement of whether the charity provided any goods or services in exchange, in whole or in part, for the gift.

A description and good-faith estimate of the value of goods or services given to the donor, if any (there is an exception for "intangible religious benefits").

When a quid pro quo contribution exceeds $75, the library must give donors a good-faith estimate of the value of the goods and services provided along with a statement that only the amount in excess of that value is deductible. An example of this would be a fund-raising event that includes a meal. The portion of the donation that covers the cost of the meal (as estimated by the library) is not deductible because the donor is getting something in return (food). Another example would be providing courtesy borrowing privileges for community borrowers (at an academic library) who make a contribution to the library. If noncontributing community borrowers must pay for borrowing privileges, then the amount that they pay for that privilege reduces the donor's deduction.

For gifts of property that total more than $500, donors must fill out Schedule A of IRS Form 8283 (Noncash Charitable Contributions) and attach it to their tax returns. The form requires the following details about the contribution:

The name and address of the library

A description of the donated property

The date of the contribution

The date the donor acquired the property and how it was acquired (by gift, purchase, etc.)

The donor's cost or other basis in the property

The method used to determine the property's fair market value

Answers to several questions regarding any restrictions attached to the gift.

Schedule B of Form 8283 is the Appraisal Summary that donors must complete if they claim a deduction for noncash charitable contributions (other than publicly traded stock) exceeding $5,000 ($10,000 in the case of stock that is not publicly traded).

The signing of Schedule B of Form 8283 triggers a filing obligation on the part of the library. In the case of gifts other than cash that have a disclosed value of $500 or more on Form 8283, the library must file Form 8282 (Donee Information Return) if it disposes of the contributed property within two years of the date of the contribution. The form need not be filed if the property is distributed without payment in exchange for it to further the library's purposes or functions.

A donor is subject to an accuracy-related penalty of 20 percent of the portion of understatement of tax to which the penalty applies. The penalty applies to substantial understatements of income tax, valuation overstatements, and negligence. Nonprofits are subject to a penalty for the failure to file a timely, complete, and accurate Form 8282.

Outright Contributions

An outright charitable contribution generally involves an immediate transfer, without reservation, of cash or property to or for the use of a qualified charitable organization.

Tax Benefits of Outright Giving

> The donor is eligible to receive a current income tax charitable deduction, generally for the full fair market value of the property.
>
> The tax savings reduce the net cost of the gift to the donor.
>
> The value of the gift (and subsequent appreciation) is excluded from the donor's estate for estate tax purposes.

Cash Gifts

Ordinary Income Property

Most types of ordinary income property (e.g., cash and some securities) can be donated to the library, yielding significant income tax deductions. For example, a donor contributes $20,000 in cash. If the donor is in the 36 percent income tax bracket, the contribution of the $20,000 to the library can reduce the donor's income tax obligation by $7,200.

Gifts of Long-Term Capital Gain Property

Generally, the deduction for a contribution of long-term capital gain property to the library is equal to the property's fair market value. Long-term capital gain property is property held for more than twelve months. A donor who contributes appreciated property to the library that does not qualify for long-term capital gain treatment is eligible to receive an income tax deduction limited to the cost basis (generally the purchase price) of the property. In other words, the income tax charitable deduction is reduced by the amount of appreciation realized during the time that the appreciated property is held.

If the donor anticipates appreciation of a capital asset, then the tax-wise approach is often to wait until the property qualifies for long-term capital gain treatment and then contribute it to the library. In contrast, if one wishes to donate securities that have declined in value, it is generally advisable to sell the securities to establish a tax loss and then donate the proceeds to the library. The donor may then be able to claim tax benefits for both the capital loss and the charitable gift, effectively deducting more than the current value of the assets.

EXAMPLE _____

Comparison of Alternative Gifting Methods

Elizabeth and John purchased 50 shares of Legacies Corporation stock in 1983 at a cost of $1,000. Today the shares are worth $5,000 and pay less than 2 percent in annual dividends.

If Elizabeth and John sold the stock, they would realize a $4,000 capital gain. Because they have held the securities long-term (for more than one year), they would owe $800 in federal capital gains tax on a sale.

Elizabeth and John, who have committed to make charitable gifts totaling $5,000 this year, normally make their gifts in the form of cash. The chart below summarizes this option and two others.

Note that the least desirable option would be to sell the stock and give away the proceeds. Giving the stock directly to the library will completely avoid the capital gains tax and the combined tax savings (capital gains plus income tax charitable deduction) is $800 cheaper than giving $5,000 in cash.

	$5k gift of cash	*Sale of stock and cash gift*	*Give securities outright*
Gift value	$5,000	$5,000	$5,000
Ordinary income tax savings	$1,980	$1,980	$1,980
Capital gains tax saved or paid assuming 20% tax rate	Not applicable	$ 800 paid	$ 800 saved
Net tax savings	**$1,980**	**$1,180**	**$2,780**

Gifts of Real Estate and Fractional Interests

A gift of appreciated real estate can be an attractive way to make a gift to the library and to realize important income and tax benefits at the same time. The donor may be able to reduce or eliminate income, capital gains, and estate taxes. The donor also may also be able to earn an income from the gift. Finally, gifting the property can relieve the donor of management worries.

The donor may deed the entire property to the library. The donor may also choose to deed an undivided fractional interest in property if the donor is not prepared to give away the entire property. The appraised value of the fractional interest is deductible for income tax purposes. Such a gift can be especially useful in providing a charitable income tax deduction to offset a capital gain generated by the subsequent sale of the entire property. Upon the sale, the donor and the library share proportionately in the proceeds.

From the library's standpoint, there is much to be concerned about in donations of real estate. There are environmental issues, easement issues, and the issue of whether the property is salable. It is always a good idea to try to ascertain whether the gift of real estate is being made out of charitable intent or whether the prospect is primarily interested in "dumping" the property. Be very wary of prospects who want to donate property to your library during the last quarter of the year when they are searching for income tax deductions!

It is the responsibility of the donor to get a qualified appraisal of the property for his or her income tax purposes. It may be prudent for the library to get an appraisal as well. This can head off surprises later on when the library seeks to sell the property. In most cases, it is also a good idea to conduct an environmental audit (a so-called stage 1 or phase 1 audit) in case there are hidden problems such as buried gas tanks or old dumpsites on the property. Your library can be liable for clean-up under the "Superfund" Clean-Up Act, and the risks and costs may far outweigh the benefits of accepting the property.

If the donation of real estate is going to be used to build a new library, then it is important to check for zoning and easement issues to make sure that the land can be used for the intended purpose. If the property is going to be sold, then the library should still have this information since it will likely affect the marketability and the purchase price.

As you can see, real estate donations require a lot of due diligence, and it is important for the library to establish written guidelines for the acceptance of real estate early on.

Special Note about Valuable Property

Undeveloped real estate, or similarly valuable but not readily salable property, often increases an individual's taxable estate without providing funds for the payment of the estate tax liability. If such property is contributed during a donor's lifetime, this estate tax liability is eliminated and the donor receives a current income tax deduction for the full fair market value of the property. An additional benefit, which is often overlooked, is that potential heirs will not be put in a position of holding property that may be difficult to manage.

Gifts of Closely Held Stock

In some cases, an individual may wish to give away closely held stock (stock that is not publicly traded on an exchange). A donor who owns highly appreciated stock in a company that has significant cash reserves (money in the bank) may be in the best position to make a significant gift.

A donor who chooses to give long-term, closely held stock outright will be able to deduct the full fair market value of the stock, up to 30 percent of the adjusted gross income, with a five-year carryforward for any excess. If the stock has appreciated in value, then the donor will also avoid the capital gains tax on the appreciation.

Another scenario is commonly referred to as a "corporate redemption" or a "stock-bailout." After the gift is made, the foundation can ask the corporation to redeem the stock at its fair market value. This will provide cash to the library, and the stock will be returned as "treasury stock" and usually "retired." Treasury stock is issued stock required by a corporation and held as an asset.

Warning! The library, the donor, the corporation, or any other party cannot be in a position to compel the purchase of the stock. This technique is often used if a donor wants to pass control to another individual or group (oftentimes children). This gift structure will serve to reduce the donor's percentage of ownership and increase the relative percentage of ownership by others, without triggering gift or estate tax.

It is possible, though complicated, to find a charitable remainder unitrust (a technique discussed later) with closely held stock.

"Buyer in the Wings"

If a donor owns stock of a corporation and a taxable takeover appears likely, the donor may contribute the stock to the library. The donor may be able to avoid the recognition of capital gain by making the contribution before the outcome of the takeover attempt is known, while gaining a tax deduction for the full fair market value of the stock.

In a recent case, *Ferguson v. Commissioner*, the Tax Court provided an excellent review of the often misunderstood assignment of income doctrine as it applies to charitable gifts. The taxpayers in *Ferguson* made charitable gifts of appreciated stock in a company that was the subject of a tender offer. A tender offer is an offer to purchase shares of stock of a corporation up to a specific number, tendered by shareholders within a specified period at a fixed price. The price is usually set at a premium above the market price. Tender offers are usually made by a party seeking to take control of a corporation and are often followed by a merger proposal.

The purchaser had acquired more than 50 percent of the stock of the company at the time that the gift was completed. Although the purchaser was not obligated to complete the purchase, the purchaser could force the completion of the sale since he or she owned more than 50 percent of the stock of the company.

The tax court held that the taxpayers did not give the stock but rather assigned expected income, because at the time of the expected gift the stock represented only a right to the future sales proceeds. To avoid the result in *Ferguson*, donors must make charitable gifts before the negotiations have progressed to a point where the purchaser can force the conclusion of the sale.

A similar analysis applies to gifts of real estate in which the donor has engaged in negotiations with a potential buyer of the property. If the donee organization sells the property to this buyer, then there is a risk that the donor will be deemed to realize the capital gain on the sale under the general theory that the donee is acting as a mere conduit for carrying out a prearranged sale. As a general rule, the donee organization should enter into independent negotiations with the buyer subsequent to the gift.

Gifts of S Corporation Stock

Amendments to the S corporation rules, which became effective on January 1, 1998, for the first time permit charitable organizations to own the stock of S corporations outright. In an S corporation (as opposed to a C corporation), shareholders may elect to have their corporation treated as a partnership for tax purposes. For all other purposes, the corporation has all of the attributes and advantages of a C corporation. A charitable remainder trust, however, may not be a shareholder in an S corporation. But the ownership of S corporation stock by charities is not without cost. The IRS says that a charity holding S corporation stock will be subject to unrelated business income taxation (the tax on income that is unrelated to the nonprofits' charitable mission), and will therefore generally be liable for the payment of some income taxes. For example, even the capital gain on the sale of the shares is subject to income tax, and is payable by the nonprofit.

The Bargain Sale

A "bargain sale" is the sale of property for less than the property's fair market value. Where such a sale is made to the library, the transaction is viewed as part sale and part charitable donation. The excess of the fair market value over the sales price is the measure of the gift to the library. The economics are illustrated in the following examples.

Bargain Sale: Securities. Donor owns appreciated long-term securities with a fair market value of $30,000 that were originally purchased for $10,000. Assume that the donor is in the 31 percent federal income tax bracket. Donor sells the securities to the library for their original cost. The $10,000 original investment is recouped. One-third of the transaction is treated as a sale, and two-thirds of the transaction is treated as a gift.

According to federal tax rules, the donor has realized a capital gain of $6,667 ($30,000 minus $10,000 times one-third) for the sale and is liable for a long-term capital gains tax of $1,333. The library then sells these securities for their full fair market value of $30,000, receiving $20,000 more than their cost. The donor is deemed to have made a charitable contribution of $20,000.

The value of the contribution is deducted in calculating the donor's taxable income, producing tax savings of $6,200. This tax savings more than offsets the $1,333 capital gains tax to which the donor is subject. The net cost of the $20,000 gift to the donor is only $15,133 ($20,000 gift plus $1,333 tax less savings of $6,200 equals $15,133).

Bargain Sale: Property Encumbered by Debt. Donor owns an interest in real estate that is worth $80,000 and that originally cost $30,000. The property is encumbered by debt of $20,000.

The donor contributes this property to the library. Because the donor's indebtedness is considered to be relieved in the charitable transaction, the bargain sale rules apply. The transfer to the library is viewed as part sale (25 percent) and part gift (75 percent). The donor incurs a long-term capital gain of $12,500 ($50,000 times 25 percent = $12,500) at the time of the gift and is liable for income tax on this gain in the amount of $2,500 (20 percent of $12,500).

The library then sells the contributed equity in the property at the net fair market value of $60,000. The donor is recognized to have made a gift of $60,000, resulting in a significant charitable income tax deduction. The value of the gift is deducted from the donor's income, producing significant income tax savings.

Deferred Giving—the Basics

Partial Interest Gifts. Generally no charitable income tax deduction is allowed for a gift of a partial interest in property. A partial interest is a gift of less than the donor's entire interest in the property. Special exceptions are made for an undivided portion of the donor's entire interest in the property, charitable remainder trusts, pooled income funds, and interests in personal residences or farms. We will explore all of these exceptions later in this chapter.

Donors to the library have the opportunity to utilize three types of life income arrangements: charitable remainder trusts (unitrust and annuity trust varieties), pooled income funds, and charitable gift annuities. The primary difference among the three vehicles is the way in which the vehicle benefits the donor(s) or such other person(s) as the donor(s) may designate before the asset passes to the library. Under any of the three arrangements, the donor(s), or the donor's designated beneficiary, is generally subject to income taxation on the income distributions. The way in which the distributions are taxed, e.g., as ordinary or capital gain income, however, varies from vehicle to vehicle. Life income arrangements may also have gift or generation-skipping tax implications, depending upon who is named as the beneficiary.

Charitable Remainder Trusts
(CRT)

A CRT allows the donor to contribute to the library while providing an income for the donor or other beneficiaries for life or for a term of years. CRTs can be tailored to suit the donor's objectives—to build a retirement account, generate a higher income from currently owned assets, or to provide for a spouse, family members, or other beneficiaries. CRTs offer a number of attractive benefits:

Increase income from low-yielding assets

Obtain immediate income tax charitable deduction

Reduce or eliminate income, gift, and estate taxes that would otherwise be due

Diversify investment assets and have the potential for tax-free growth of assets

Create a source of income for children, parents, or other loved ones

Enjoy making a gift to the library that might not otherwise be possible

Charitable Remainder Annuity Trust (CRAT)

The CRAT, in contrast to the CRUT, pays the income beneficiary a fixed annual income determined at the outset, irrespective of the amount of income actually earned by the trust. The annual payment to the income beneficiary must be a minimum of 5 percent of the value of the assets determined at the time the trust is created. The annuity trust may be advantageous if the donor is more interested in the security of a constant return than in the long-term growth potential of the charitable remainder. Additions may not be made to a CRAT (as with a CRUT); however, multiple trusts can be established.

EXAMPLE

Charitable Remainder Annuity Trust

If the donors in the CRUT example (see p. 54) establish a CRAT, their annual payment is fixed at $21,000 (7 percent of $300,000). Here are some other differences between the CRAT and the CRUT: Over the projected 33-year term of the CRAT, assuming an 8 percent total return within the trust, the projected pretax benefit to donors is $693,000 (versus $816,000 with the CRUT). The projected nominal value of the benefit to the library is $738,000 with the CRAT and $417,000 with the CRUT. The income tax charitable deduction is the same for both forms of trust, approximately $49,400 (see the following chart).

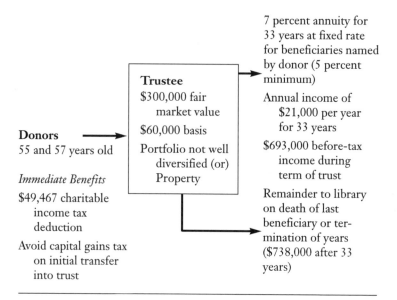

Charitable remainder trusts (CRTs) can be used creatively to help the philanthropically inclined achieve both philanthropic and financial objectives. For example, a donor who is concerned about college costs for children or grandchildren might want to design a charitable remainder trust for a period of time up to twenty years, as circumstances require.

EXAMPLE

Mrs. Bernstein, 69, has a granddaughter, Rebecca, who is beginning college next year. She promised many years ago that she would help Rebecca with her college expenses. She has mutual funds that have increased in value over the years but yield very little income.

Mrs. Bernstein sets up a CRT that will last for the four years that Rebecca is in college. The trust will be funded with the mutual funds, which will be sold free of capital gains tax and reinvested in a way that will produce a greater total return.

Each year Rebecca will receive a fixed sum from earnings of the trust or from principal, if necessary. Mrs. Bernstein's income tax charitable deduction will be large because the trust lasts for such a short period of time.

Testamentary CRTs (those that become effective at one's death) do not qualify for an income tax charitable deduction. They do, however, entitle the donor to a dollar-for-dollar estate tax charitable deduction.

The Taxpayer Relief Act of 1997 imposed additional requirements on charitable remainder trusts. In order to prevent certain abuses of charitable remainder trusts for primarily noncharitable purposes, Congress imposed two additional requirements for a qualifying charitable remainder trust:

> The payout from a charitable remainder trust (whether a unitrust or an annuity trust) may not exceed 50 percent. This amendment is effective for transfers made after June 18, 1997.

> The actuarial value of the remainder interest (determined under Internal Revenue Code Section 7520) must be at least 10 percent of the initial fair market value of the property placed in trust. This amendment is effective for transfers made after July 28, 1997.

These new rules have a number of practical implications, among them: (1) It is necessary to review all testamentary instruments creating charitable remainder trusts or providing for further transfers to trusts to make certain that trusts qualify; and (2) The 10 percent rule will have a limiting effect on trusts for children if the children are relatively young. Qualification, of course, also becomes more difficult as the number of beneficiaries increases.

Table 3.1 on page 54 shows the maximum payout rates that could be used for a single individual and for a married couple using an applicable federal rate of 7.6 percent. The applicable federal rate, or AFR, is a percentage rate that the IRS publishes monthly. It is a rate used in calculating charitable deductions for charitable remainder trusts, pooled income funds, charitable gift annuities, and charitable lead trusts. In most cases, donors can elect to use the rate for the month in which the gift is made or either of the two preceding months.

The Taxpayer Relief Act of 1997 specifies that the charitable tax deduction (the present value of the charity's remainder interest in a charitable remainder trust) must be 10 percent of the value of the assets contributed to the trust. Table 3.1 assumes an applicable federal rate of 7.6 percent.

Because the minimum percentage for payouts from CRTs is 5 percent, once the payout rate reaches 5 percent no further benefit is allowed.

Table 3.1 Single Life Trust

Age	Maximum Payout Rate (%)	Ages	Two-Life Trust (%)
80	50	80/80	26
75	39	75/75	20
70	30	70/70	15
65	23	65/65	12
60	17	60/60	10
55	14	55/55	8
50	11	50/50	7
45	9	45/45	6
40	7	40/40	5
35	6	35/35	5
30	5	30/30	N/A

Charitable Remainder Unitrusts (CRUT)

With a CRUT, the donor transfers property in trust, reserves a variable annuity interest for a noncharitable beneficiary, and contributes the remainder interest in the property to the library. CRUTs must pay the noncharitable beneficiary a fixed percentage (not less than 5 percent) of the net fair market value of the trust assets, valued annually. The term of the trust must be a term of years (not exceeding twenty) or the life or lives of the noncharitable beneficiary. Additions to a CRUT are permissible.

EXAMPLE

Charitable Remainder Unitrust

Donors are 57 and 55 years old, and they own a portfolio of publicly traded stock that they accumulated during their marriage. The portfolio, which is not particularly well diversified, has a present value of $300,000 and a cost basis of 20 percent or $60,000. The stocks pay dividends of 1 percent, or $3,000 per year, and the donors wish to generate substantial additional income.

Donors contribute the stock to a CRUT. They reserve the right to receive 7 percent of the trust's annual value during their joint lifetimes, with the unitrust payments to continue during the survivor's lifetime. Following the survivor's death, the trust will be distributed to a memorial fund established at the library. Donors will receive an immediate income tax deduction, based on their ages, of $49,467.

Because the stocks are contributed to the charitable remainder unitrust before they are sold, the trustee's sale avoids capital gains taxes. Accordingly, the pretax balance of the proceeds ($300,000) can be invested for total return (in a well-diversified portfolio of equity and debt instruments). Donors will now have an initial annual income of $21,000 (7 percent of $300,000), rather than $3,000 per year (1 percent of $300,000). The annual income in subsequent years will fluctuate depending upon the value of the trust investments. Assuming that the trust assets grow by 8 percent per year (a very conservative assumption), donors will receive a total of $816,249 during the 33-year term of the trust. At the death of the surviving spouse, the unitrust assets will pass to the library with no estate tax. The benefit to the library is $416,607 (see the chart below).

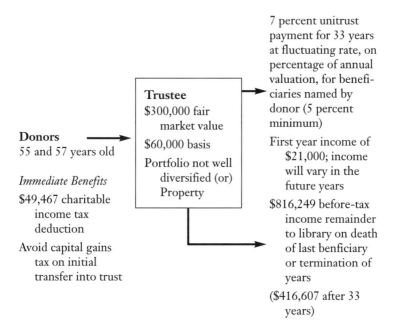

7 percent unitrust payment for 33 years at fluctuating rate, on percentage of annual valuation, for beneficiaries named by donor (5 percent minimum)

First year income of $21,000; income will vary in the future years

$816,249 before-tax income remainder to library on death of last benficiary or termination of years

($416,607 after 33 years)

Trustee
$300,000 fair market value
$60,000 basis
Portfolio not well diversified (or)
Property

Donors
55 and 57 years old

Immediate Benefits
$49,467 charitable income tax deduction

Avoid capital gains tax on initial transfer into trust

By comparison, if donors had sold the portfolio of securities for $300,000, they would have paid a capital gains tax of $48,000, leaving after-tax proceeds of $252,000 to be invested. At 7 percent, the $252,000 would have produced an initial annual income of $17,640, which is less than the income available to the donors from the CRUT. The CRUT also may reduce donors' estate tax liability.

Unitrusts: Variations on a Theme

There are four ways to arrange the structure of payments from a CRUT.

Regular Unitrust: Payments fluctuate with the value of assets or earnings of the trust. Trust principal may be used ("invaded") to make the payments if there is insufficient income to do so.

Net Income Unitrust: Unitrust payment is the net income from the trust or the stated percentage, whichever is less.

Net Income Unitrust with Makeup Provision: The donor receives all of the benefits of the Net Income Unitrust; later, if the trust assets produce income that exceeds the payout amount specified in the trust, the donor can catch up by exceeding the payout specified in the trust until this "IOU" account is paid off.

FLIP Unitrust: Unitrust starts with an income or net income limitation with makeup that will "flip" to become a regular unitrust after the occurrence of an event that is not within the control of the trustee or any other person(s), e.g., marriage, divorce, birth, death, or one's sixty-fifth birthday. This relatively new device is especially useful in situations when the asset funding the trust is not readily marketable, such as real estate.

Two Common Misperceptions about Charitable Remainder Trusts

1. *Trust Beneficiaries Always Receive Tax-Free Income.* The CRT is itself a tax-exempt entity, so it can *sell* highly appreciated assets without being taxed on the capital gain or ordinary income. This allows the

donor to trade one type of asset for another. Distributions to beneficiaries, however, are subject to income taxation under a somewhat complicated "four-tier" (some say four tear!) system. The beneficiaries are taxed on the payments they receive in the following order: Ordinary income, capital gains, other income including tax-exempt income, and principal.

Therefore, it is not possible for a donor to (a) create a charitable remainder trust with appreciated securities; (b) avoid capital gain taxes; (c) get a charitable income tax deduction; and (d) have the trust reinvest in tax-exempt securities and pay out tax-exempt income. Any capital gain on the sale of the securities will not be taxed to the charitable remainder trust. Rather, it will *pass through* and be taxable to the noncharitable beneficiary before any tax-exempt income can be paid out.

It is possible to structure a CRT to pay the income beneficiary tax-exempt income. Such a trust can initially be funded with cash or tax-exempt bonds.

2. It Is Acceptable to Fund a CRT with Encumbered Property. Donors should *not* contribute encumbered real property to a charitable remainder trust for a number of fairly technical tax reasons. The main planning options are to pay off the debt or attempt to substitute other security, so that the property funding the CRT is unencumbered.

Pooled Income Fund (PIF)

Donors making smaller gifts can avoid the expense of setting up a separate trust (a CRT) by using a PIF. This charitable fund is distinguished from CRT arrangements by one main feature: Similar to mutual funds, the donor participates in a larger fund composed of numerous individuals' donations that are pooled for the purpose of investment. The yield varies from year to year. Unlike CRTs, these funds may not be invested in tax-exempt securities. Following is a summary of PIF features.

As with a CRUT, the donor may make additions to his or her original gift at future times, and like both forms of CRT, the donor may designate a person other than himself or herself to be the income beneficiary.

Each donor is assigned shares based on the value of the gift in relation to the entire fund (see figure 3.2).

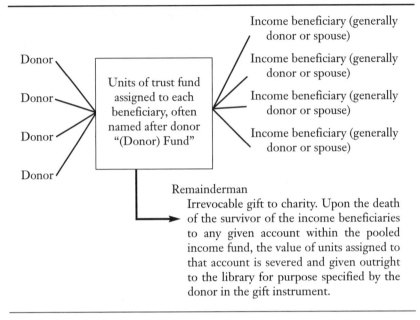

Figure 3.2 Fund Held by Trustee

At the death of the beneficiary, the balance of the donated assets in the PIF flows to the library.

The donor's income is taxed as ordinary income.

The income tax benefits of participation in a pooled income fund are similar to those available to donors who create a CRT.

You may be able to establish a PIF for the benefit of the library through your local community foundation, which will likely charge an administration fee (typically 1 percent per year).

Remainder Interest in Personal Residence or Farm

A charitable donation can be made to the library of a remainder interest in an individual's home, with the donor retaining a lifetime right to live in or on the property. The term *home* is defined by the IRS as any property that is used as a personal residence, even though it need not be the donor's principal residence, and encompasses the donor's vacation home, motor home, or even a boat. Farms are also eligible.

The donor is entitled to any income that the property produces and is responsible for its upkeep. An income tax charitable deduction is available in the year of the gift equal to the value of the remainder interest (the amount that the library will eventually receive). When the donor dies, the library receives the property (as shown in the chart).

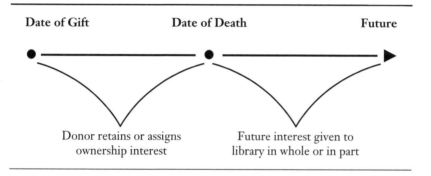

| **Date of Gift** | **Date of Death** | **Future** |

Donor retains or assigns ownership interest

Future interest given to library in whole or in part

Charitable Gift Annuities (CGA)

A charitable gift annuity is similar to a commercial annuity purchased from a life insurance company, except that the purchase price includes a combination of the value of the future annuity payments and a contribution to the charity issuing the annuity. Since the transaction is partially a charitable contribution, the amount of the annuity payment will be less than that obtained from a commercial insurance company. Most nonprofits issue CGAs using payout rates established by the American Council on Gift Annuities. These rates are set so that, on average, the nonprofit will receive 50 percent of the initial contribution. On the other hand, the purchaser of the annuity will receive a current income tax charitable deduction. Obviously, this is not the case with commercial annuities. Here are some sample payout rates for single life annuities: 7.5 percent for a 70-year-old, 8.2 percent for a 75-year-old, 9.2 percent for an 80-year-old. Donors 90 and over receive a payout of 12 percent. A joint and survivor annuity, e.g., husband and wife, where the younger donor is 80 and the older donor is 84 would receive an 8.3 percent payout.

The advantages of charitable gift annuities include

accommodation of smaller gifts

annual payments fixed at the outset so income is predictable

beneficial taxation of annuity payments (tax-free return of principal)

capital gains often distributed over the life of the annuity

current income tax charitable deduction

annuity payments *guaranteed* by the charity's assets. This feature is particularly attractive to many prospective donors.

Charitable gift annuity programs are often carefully regulated, and some states regulate them more heavily than others. It can take many months to set up a charitable gift annuity program. Academic libraries have an advantage over public libraries if their university already has a charitable gift annuity program in place. As with PIFs, your library may wish to discuss utilizing the charitable gift annuity program of a local community foundation.

EXAMPLE _____

Immediate Payment Charitable Gift Annuity

Mrs. Cox, 80, has decided to make several gifts through her will and other long-range plans. She would actually like to make those gifts now, but has decided that she cannot do so because she may need income from her assets for future living expenses.

After learning about CGAs, however, she decides to make a gift of $20,000 in cash. At her age, she will receive annual payments of $1,840, or 9.2 percent of the amount transferred, for as long as she lives, no matter what the earnings are from the amount used to pay for the annuity. For the first nine years of her payments, she will not pay federal income tax on $732 of the payment she receives—it is considered a tax-free return of principal. Afterwards, she will pay tax on the remaining amount of the payment as well. Additional tax benefits include an income tax charitable deduction of about $10,000 in the year in which the gift is completed and removal of the amount used to fund the CGA, plus appreciation, from Mrs. Cox's estate (see the following chart).

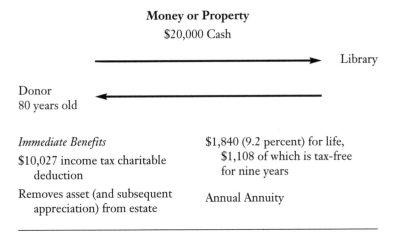

Money or Property
$20,000 Cash

Library

Donor
80 years old

Immediate Benefits	$1,840 (9.2 percent) for life,
$10,027 income tax charitable deduction	$1,108 of which is tax-free for nine years
Removes asset (and subsequent appreciation) from estate	Annual Annuity

A creative gift planning idea for donors in the 25- to 55-age range is the deferred payment charitable gift annuity. This giving vehicle can be structured like an IRA (individual retirement account). Deferred gift annuities are beneficial to younger donors, especially younger donors who are working and do not need more income immediately. They are also beneficial to donors who run the risk of over-funding their IRAs or other qualified retirement plans. The donor's income is deferred usually until age 65. Some of the characteristics of deferred gift annuities include

If the younger donor is willing to wait until age 65 or older for income, the donor can receive a very high yearly rate of return.

Donors receive an immediate income tax charitable deduction based on their age and the time when they receive their first payment.

The donor has earnings sheltered with a compounded return, similar to an IRA.

The donor has the opportunity to make a large gift early in life and can play a meaningful role in the charitable community while still young.

The deferred income to retirement age is partially tax free, and the taxable income is likely to be taxed at a lower rate.

EXAMPLE _____

Deferred Payment Charitable Gift Annuity

Mr. Bernstein's son, David, 50, transfers $20,000 in cash to the library for a deferred gift annuity with the payments to start at age 65. Based on his age, David will receive a guaranteed annual payment of 16.4 percent, or $3,280. He qualifies for a $12,170 income tax charitable deduction in the year of the gift, and $420 of each payment made to him will be tax-free for his life expectancy (until he reaches the age of 83, according to IRS mortality tables). David can build a sizable retirement fund by creating a new CGA each year.

Charitable Lead Trust (CLT)

The charitable lead trust is the opposite of a charitable remainder trust, allowing the donor to make a future transfer of assets to heirs at a highly reduced or "zeroed out" transfer tax cost, while continuing to support the library during the donor's lifetime. During a specified number of years, a variable or fixed percentage of the trust assets are paid to the library. At the end of the trust term, the assets flow to the noncharitable beneficiary named by the donor (typically children).

The short-term and long-term benefits for the donor's estate can be significant. First, the donor can receive a gift tax charitable deduction for the value today of the annual trust payments that the library will receive over time. This deduction can be used to reduce or eliminate the donor's gift or estate tax liability on substantial transfers to children or grandchildren. The donor should check with his or her professional advisor(s) regarding the potential generation-skipping transfer tax implications of a trust established for the benefit of grandchildren or others.

Although the donor will generally not receive an income tax charitable deduction, a second advantage of the CLT is that the income earned by the trust is excluded from the donor's gross income and is, therefore, not taxable to the donor. In effect, this reduces the donor's taxes over the trust term.

A third attractive aspect of the charitable lead trust is that any appreciation in asset value during the term of the trust is not subject to additional gift or estate taxation. As a result, the donor may be able to pass on to heirs a significantly larger estate after taxes than would otherwise be possible.

To qualify as a CLT, the trust must be created in either the form of an annuity trust or a unitrust (defined in the same way as for CRTs). Additionally, CLTs can be funded either during the donor's lifetime or in a testamentary fashion. The example illustrates the potential tax advantages of a CLT for transferring property to heirs.

EXAMPLE _____

Charitable Lead Trust

Donor is preparing an updated estate plan and wishes to make a substantial gift for the benefit of her grandchildren, none of whom is presently over the age of 35. Donor also wishes to make a substantial gift for the benefit of the library. Donor's estate plan is revised to include a charitable lead annuity trust, which is to be funded with $500,000 in assets at donor's death. The trust will pay the library $25,000 per year (5 percent) for 20 years, creating an endowment fund to benefit several library programs and services. After 20 years, the entire trust balance will be distributed to the donor's grandchildren.

The Charitable Lead Annuity Trust will result in an estate tax charitable deduction of 53 percent of the original contribution of $500,000 or $264,850. Moreover, the trust will be fully exempt from generation-skipping transfer taxes, because the donor can apply $500,000 of the $1 million generation-skipping transfer tax exemption to this trust. If the trust grows at a rate of 2 percent more than the $25,000 payments to the library, the amount ultimately to be distributed to the donor's grandchildren at the end of 20 years will be $803,923, even though the estate tax value of the trust at the date of donor's death was only $264,850, as shown in the following chart.

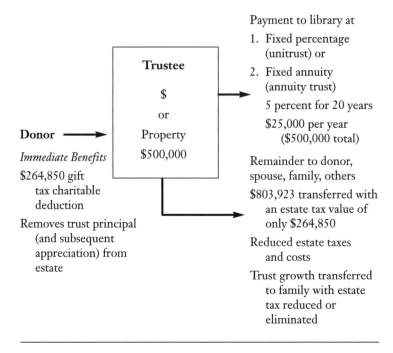

Special notes regarding charitable lead trusts: Estate tax rates of up to 55 percent (60 percent if the excise tax on very large estates applies) make the net cost after tax of the yearly income relinquished by the donor relatively small for taxpayers in high brackets.

For a lead trust to work successfully, the asset(s) selected by the donor to fund the trust must be selected carefully. It is most advantageous for a donor to use property with a high potential for appreciation in value to fund the lead trust.

Charitable Bequests
(Wills/Living Trusts)

A will is a legal document in which a person states various binding intentions about what he or she wants done with his or her property after death. It is a statement about what matters most in life. By making a will, one can ensure that his or her intentions are clearly expressed and will be followed by those administering his or her estate.

After providing for family, friends, and others (if desired), many alumni and Friends include a meaningful gift to the library in order to continue their lifetime support. Bequests can take several forms:

A specified dollar amount

Specific assets

A percentage of the estate. A donor can leave the library a percentage of the estate, or of an asset in the estate, such as part of a ranch or a percentage of the residuary estate. This type of bequest automatically adjusts with fluctuations in the total amount passing under a will. It is therefore protected against inflation and almost always assures the library of some charitable gift.

Residual bequest. This is a gift of all or part of the estate to the library after all of the general bequests (from the general assets of the estate, generally cash) and specific bequests (e.g., a grandfather clock or 100 shares of IBM stock) have been distributed. The residue is "what's left."

Contingent bequest. This takes effect only if the other provisions can't be satisfied, e.g., if all of the children predecease the parents, or die in a common disaster, e.g., an airplane crash.

The following sample provisions may be helpful in planning a bequest:

Unrestricted Bequests

I give [describe dollar amount, property to be given, percentage of estate or proportion of residuary estate] to Smithtown Public Library, a nonprofit corporation with its principal offices in Smithtown, California, in the County of Jonesville, to be used for the general purposes of the library in the discretion of its board.

Restricted Bequests

I give [describe dollar amount, property to be given, percentage of estate or proportion of residuary estate] to Smithtown Public Library, a nonprofit corporation with its principal offices in Smithtown, California, in the County of Jonesville, for the following restricted purpose [indicate purpose]. For example, one can structure a bequest so that it is held in an endowment fund with the annual distribution amount used to purchase children's literature.

Tax Benefits

With either form of bequest, the taxable portion of the donor's estate is reduced by the entire fair market value of the bequest. No limitations are imposed by federal tax rules on the amount that may be deducted and no distinction is made between ordinary income property and capital gain property. Note that the only other unlimited deduction in the federal tax law is for transfers between spouses.

The estate tax savings reduce the net cost of the gift to the donor's estate. Estate taxes range from 37 percent to 55 percent.

Other Benefits

The donor may change his or her mind and revoke a bequest, though this rarely happens. Charitable bequests are an excellent way for donors to provide for the library without parting with income during their lifetime. Donors should be encouraged to share their plans so that the library will have an opportunity to acknowledge their thoughtfulness and generosity (and to track "bequest expectancies").

Just as in the case of a gift by will, a donor can provide for eventual gifts of cash, securities, property, or other assets through a revocable living trust. The gift is revocable during the donor's lifetime.

Since gifts through trusts (and wills) can be revoked (the donor can change his or her mind), there are no income tax advantages. However, the donor is able to arrange a charitable gift without risk to his or her financial future.

Title to the property passes under the terms of the trust agreement. It does not pass through the donor's will and may avoid the possible costs and delays often associated with probate.

During the donor's lifetime, the income from the donor's trust will be paid to the donor or to another person or nonprofit organization as directed by the donor. Many attorneys recommend that the trust agreement explicitly authorize the trustee of the trust (which may be the donor) to distribute assets to a nonprofit.

EXAMPLE _____

A mother's final tribute to her daughter's lifelong devotion was a generous bequest to the Monroe University Library. Dianne Smith was the mother of Carol Jones, a 1952 graduate in library science. Mrs. Smith proudly watched her daughter's lifetime successes, including Carol's baccalaureate years at Monroe. Carol loved to read, and she spent almost all of her free time at the library.

Carol Jones was devoted to her mother, and her mother reciprocated this devotion. Their wills had been written identically: each left her entire estate to the other, with the knowledge that the survivor would then make a generous bequest to Monroe University.

Jones died before her mother and, as planned, her estate went to ensure her mother's security and well-being. Mrs. Smith passed away in 1991 and, as a poignant farewell to her daughter, she made a bequest of 25 percent of her estate, which will benefit the library. The beneficence of this proud and devoted mother will help to ensure the continued strength of the library's programs and services.

Retirement Plans

Retirement plans such as IRAs, Keoghs, and qualified plans (including defined benefit and defined contribution plans) are excellent tax and financial planning devices, but various taxes may cause shrinkage of 70 percent or more when the remaining dollars are transferred to the participant's heirs upon death. A significant percentage of a prospect's estate may be tied up in retirement plans (in the authors' experience, this is especially true of doctors!).

EXAMPLE _____

Sally and Roger are planning to make a bequest to your library. They also want to provide for their grandson. It is often a good idea to make the charitable gift using regular IRA funds instead of other assets. Distributions from IRAs are taxable as ordinary income, but bequests of other assets are tax free to heirs.

For example, if Sally and Roger leave $100,000 in a regular IRA to their grandson, who is in the 40 percent income tax bracket (federal and state combined), the grandson will receive only $60,000 if he cashes in the IRA. But if Sally and Roger instead bequeath $100,000 in cash, their grandson will receive the cash tax free. And if they bequeath appreciated property worth $100,000, their grandson can sell it with a stepped-up basis to obtain $100,000 in cash without paying a capital gains tax.

Of course, charities such as the library pay no income tax and can receive IRA distributions tax free. So by leaving an IRA to the library—and other property to the grandson, instead of the reverse, they cut the IRS out of their estate.

The way to leave an IRA to the library is simply to name it as a beneficiary.

Taxes

The following taxes may affect the distribution of assets held in retirement plans.

Income tax. Distributions from most retirement accounts are subject to federal income taxation. If the participant makes a withdrawal during his or her lifetime, the income tax will be payable at whatever rates apply in the year of distribution. Currently income tax rates are as high as 39.6 percent. If a beneficiary receives a distribution after the participant's death, it is taxed to the beneficiary at the beneficiary's income tax rate. If the retirement account is payable to the participant's estate, the entire distribution will be subject to income taxation (payable by the estate). If a surviving spouse is named as the beneficiary, the spouse may be eligible to rollover the distribution to an IRA, continuing to defer the income tax. The planning issue, then, becomes what happens upon the death of the surviving spouse? One creative solution is remarriage—making another rollover possible!

Estate tax. The value of retirement plan assets is also subject to the federal estate tax. If the plan assets are payable to the surviving spouse or a qualifying trust for the benefit of the surviving spouse, then the assets can qualify for the unlimited marital deduction.

Generation-skipping tax. The "generation-skipping transfer tax," currently a flat 55 percent tax, can apply if a distribution is made to a "skip person" not protected by the participant's $1 million generation-skipping transfer tax exemption. A skip person is a beneficiary who is two or more generations younger than the participant.

As shown in the preceding example, the combined impact of the estate and income taxes alone on retirement funds can dramatically reduce the net benefits anticipated by the participant and his or her beneficiaries. Because of the significant tax burden that can be imposed on retirement plans, these assets can provide a tax-wise gift to the library for charitably minded individuals.

Retirement planning is a top priority for more and more people as longevity increases, investment returns fluctuate, and the number of people considering retirement needs grows. It is no surprise, then, that there are charitable vehicles that prospective donors might consider to address these issues (especially outright gifts upon death, testamentary charitable remainder unitrusts, discussed below, and deferred charitable gift annuities, which were discussed previously in this chapter). There are several charitable possibilities. (Donors should discuss non-charitable options with their professional advisors.)

Bequest to the library. Designating the library as the beneficiary of the retirement plan will eliminate both the income tax and the estate tax. One important caution: the amount distributed may be the entire amount or a fractional portion—not a fixed amount. To distribute a fixed amount, the estate must recognize in full the ordinary income for the amount specified and the income tax will not be avoided.

In order to implement such a plan, the donor need only ask the plan administrator for a change of beneficiary form and indicate the fractional portion or percentage of assets he or she wishes to distribute to the library. The consent of a spouse may be necessary in some instances.

Testamentary charitable remainder unitrust. Plan assets can be transferred to a Charitable Remainder Unitrust (CRUT) upon the death of the participant. The CRUT would then distribute income to the beneficiary selected by the participant for a specified time period, with the remainder passing to the library. The advantages of this technique include

> There will be an estate tax charitable deduction equal to the value today of the amount of money that will eventually pass to the library. This reduces (but does not eliminate) the donor's estate tax liability.

There will be no income taxes payable on the retirement assets at the time of the distribution to the CRUT.

The appreciation on the retirement assets is not subject to income tax when distributed to the CRT.

Because of the tax savings, the income beneficiaries may enjoy a stream of income from a larger fund using the CRUT than if they had received the after tax value of the retirement assets outright.

A more thorough discussion of charitable remainder unitrusts is presented earlier in this chapter.

Withdrawal plus unitrust contribution. An interesting strategy to consider (though it is rarely used) is withdrawing funds during the participant's lifetime, paying income tax, and then contributing the proceeds to a CRUT. The income tax deduction on the contribution to the CRUT will in part offset the ordinary income realized on the withdrawal. It may be possible to preserve up to 60 percent or 70 percent of the withdrawn amount for contribution to the CRUT.

Life Insurance

Life insurance can be a valuable asset for accomplishing an individual's philanthropic objectives at a relatively small net cost. For example, a donor can

Donate a paid-up policy (no more premiums are due) originally purchased to satisfy a need that no longer exists; e.g., a spouse who will no longer need the policy, a child who is now a financially independent adult, a policy to complete the payment of a mortgage already paid in full, or a policy to provide for a child's education when that education has already been paid for from other assets. The donor irrevocably designates the library as the owner and the beneficiary of the policy. The donor is entitled to an income tax charitable deduction equal to the "replacement" value or tax cost basis, whichever is less.

Give away a policy that is not fully paid up and take a deduction for the present value of the policy (approximately the cash surrender value or cost basis, whichever is less). If the donor then continues to make premium payments, they are deductible for income tax purposes.

Take out a new policy and transfer ownership to the library. The donor's premium payments will be tax deductible.

Life insurance is often used as a wealth replacement asset. The donor donates property to the library and replaces the dollar value of the asset with life insurance for his or her heirs. The income tax savings from the donor's gift may be sufficient to pay the premiums for the life insurance. Through this arrangement, the donor may be able to replace an illiquid asset (such as a residence) that would be subject to estate taxes with a highly liquid asset (the insurance policy) that can pass tax free to the donor's heirs. In many states, e.g., Arizona, California, Connecticut, Kentucky, and Maine, statutes expressly permit a nonprofit organization to own an insurance policy on the life of an individual. In New York, on the other hand, a nonprofit organization generally does not have an "insurable interest" in the life of an individual. But an individual in New York, on his or her own initiative, may purchase a life insurance policy on his or her life that he or she subsequently donates. The advice of qualified counsel is important in this area of charitable gift planning.

Putting It All Together:
Some Typical Donor Profiles

While planned giving is a highly individualized process, there are nevertheless several types of prospects who fit a certain pattern in terms of their philanthropic and financial objectives. Here are some fairly typical charitable gift plans.

1. *The Annual Giver.* What happens when a Friend of the library dies? Who will replace this annual gift? A bequest is often the best technique to ensure that the gift will last in perpetuity. The donor is asked to leave a gift at his or her death to the library that is equal to twenty times above his or her average annual gift. This gift is expected to earn income at the annual rate of 5 percent, which will generate the same annual gift after the donor's death as the donor made during his or her lifetime. Excess income is added to the principal, so gifts should increase each year, depending on investment results.

2. *The Older Donor.* The goal of many seniors is to reduce management responsibilities and increase cash flow on low yielding assets. A charitable gift annuity can often accomplish these objectives. The best prospects for charitable gift annuities are individuals or couples who are 65 years of age or older. The assets must be marketable and the library should be able to sell them. Assets may have mortgages or debts against them (unlike CRTs), but, when gifted, the amount of the debt transferred will be considered as a cash payment to the donor and taxable immediately to him or her.

3. *The Intermediate Donor.* This donor tends to be between 45 and 65 years old, owns some appreciated stocks or bonds, and is interested in increased income, some tax benefits, and more diversification. Their assets tend to be worth between $5,000 and $50,000, with substantial appreciation in value. A pooled income fund may be the answer in this scenario. The donor will receive an immediate income tax charitable deduction, elimination of the capital gains tax, cash flow for life, diversification, professional investment management, and the satisfaction of making a significant gift to the library.

4. *Major Planned Gifts.* Following are typical scenarios for major planned gifts.

> *Prospect 1:* This type of donor tends to be between 60 and 75 years old, although the planning concepts are available to both older and younger donors. The donor owns a highly appreciated asset that is underproductive or that he or she intends to sell. This might apply to raw land, rental real estate, a closely held business, or publicly traded stock. The donor seeks to avoid the capital gains tax and maintain and maximize the income from the sale proceeds.

> *Prospect 2:* This donor is about 50 years old, a high earner and eager to accumulate wealth in a tax-free environment. Donor's pension plan is overfunded.

A charitable remainder trust can work well for both Prospects 1 and 2.

> *Prospect 3:* This donor tends to be between 60 and 75 years old, although the planning concepts are available to both older and younger donors. The donor owns a highly appreciated asset that is also productive and that he or she wants to keep in the family. This might apply to real estate or a closely held business. The

donor seeks to avoid transfer taxes in passing the asset to heirs, and the donor also wants to help the library.

A charitable lead trust can work well for Prospect 3.

Prospect 4: The donor is 75 years old or older, owns a highly appreciated house, and either has little in the way of other assets or has substantial other wealth.

A life estate agreement ("gift or sale of a remainder interest in a personal residence or farm") can work well for Prospect 4.

Conclusion

Nobody expects librarians to comprehend the complex tax laws governing planned giving. That is the job of other professionals who are part of the planned-giving team. Nevertheless, a familiarity with the names of the charitable gift planning vehicles, and how they can help to solve tax and financial problems, is an achievable goal. If you can recognize the "door openers to planned giving," and can speak articulately once the door is open, significant gifts *will* result, over time.

Once the door is open, the primary role of the librarian is to help the prospective donor develop his or her "philanthropic vision." How will the dollars be used? What impact will they have, both on the library and on the donor? The vision always comes before the vehicle, so helping the prospect develop an articulate philanthropic vision is crucial. Those who do not have "donative intent" are unlikely to give for one simple reason: it generally costs something to give assets away. As we have seen, the charitable gift planning process can significantly reduce the cost of giving, but not to nothing.

Saving taxes generally does not cause a person to give. Saving taxes provides an additional incentive for those who have already chosen to give, and may allow them to make a larger gift than they ever dreamed possible. Planned gifts are generally "nonrecurring." They happen once in a lifetime or are funded "on the installment plan." They are large gifts and can make a tremendous impact on the quality of your library's offerings. All members of the charitable gift planning team have a unique role to play, and collectively they can help make your library the best that it can be. Always remember that while your role is vital, there are many other supportive players on the team.

4

Components of a
Planned-Giving Strategy

A successful planned-giving program moves along a continuum from finding potential donors to administering the eventual gifts. There is much work, and many years, between these points.

Identifying Prospects

A fund-raising dictionary would define "prospect" as a potential donor. It is up to you to identify the potential donors to your library, and that is called "identifying prospects." This is the first step of a planned-giving program.

We believe that libraries, like hospitals with grateful patients, have a natural group of prospects. Planned-giving prospects can be found in your Friends group, may volunteer in your library, may be regular patrons, or may already be donors. Trustees, current and retired board members, current or retired staff and faculty, and attendees at library events and programs are also great sources of planned-giving prospects. Usually your prospects are self-identified by their commitment to, and affiliation with, your library.

Demographics

Planned-giving prospects differ from ordinary donors, although ordinary donors can certainly become planned-giving donors. The generally accepted planned-giving donor profile is a prospect 55 years of age or older. The stereotypical planned-giving prospect is a wealthy widow, over 70, with no direct heirs. The salient feature of these profiles is age.

Because planned-giving has aspects of estate, tax, and financial planning, chances are the prospects have accumulated enough wealth to be concerned about preserving it, transferring it, and hopefully giving some of it to institutions that have meant much to them during their lifetime.

Childless and single prospects usually do not have immediate family members to transfer their wealth to and therefore look to the institutions that could benefit from their accumulated wealth. Widows or widowers, with or without children, may be interested in honoring a deceased spouse by establishing an endowment gift.

Even prospects with children should be considered planned-giving prospects. In some cases, donors with accumulated wealth will take care of family members and still feel they have enough to give to meaningful institutions. Some donors may not want to give all their wealth to their children for fear of stifling incentive in them to achieve their own success. In other cases, the children may not need their parents' wealth, and that frees the donors to give elsewhere. There are many scenarios out there, so it is important to keep an open mind when "prospecting" for planned-giving donors.

Identifying donors can be done in different ways. As I mentioned earlier, most prospects are self-identified by their interest in your library, demonstrated either by earlier donations, by joining your Friends groups, by volunteering in your library, by serving on your board, or by functioning as a regular and supportive patron.

Some of these self-identified prospects may also be donors elsewhere in the community, so it is important to try to determine where your library ranks among the prospect's charitable interests. It is probably not unusual to have a person who is a major donor by your standards but actually gives more to other institutions in your community.

It is helpful to have a sense of your prospects' charitable giving in the community at large. One way to do this is to pay attention to the donor recognition literature from the other major institutions in your community. For example, study the donor wall when you go to the museum or read closely the donor recognition page of the symphony program. By doing this, you will get a sense of where your prospects are giving; often the recognition vehicles from these other institutions indicate level of giving as well.

Another method of identifying prospects is through friends and contacts. If your library is serious about seeking planned gifts and you go so far as forming a planned gifts advisory board, the members of the board can be extremely helpful in identifying prospects. In fact, the members of the board should be prepared to identify prospects as part of their responsibilities of serving on the board. Often community members who serve on boards and committees are tied into a network of givers (and doers) and can share important information on prospects. The underlying role of fund-raising committee or board members is "give or get."

Another method is to join local fund-raising organizations such as the National Society of Fund Raising Executives (NSFRE) or the local chapter of the National Committee on Planned Gifts (NCPG). Joining these organizations can be helpful on many levels. The goals of these organizations are to educate and share information. Some information that is shared is about local philanthropists, which can be helpful to you in determining who your prospects are and where else they give in the community. See chapter 5 for more on the benefits of joining these organizations.

Cultivation

The cultivation process begins after you have qualified the prospect— that is, have a sense of the prospect's charitable intent and whether the person has money or property to give, and you have determined that the person's affiliation or history with your library ranks high on his or her list of institutions to support.

During the cultivation period, it is also helpful to get a sense of the motivation of your prospects. Do they wish to honor someone? Are they grateful for something the library did? Do they wish to establish a collection or an endowment, or support a library program? Are they seeking financial or tax benefits, prestige, or status? Or are they seeking recognition? Do the prospects have long-term financial goals, and can your library help with those goals? Are you being realistic?

All fund-raising, and especially planned giving, is based on relationships. In fact, the relationship is the key. To have a successful planned-giving program, you must establish relationships that are based on trust and communication. Prospects must be assured of confidentiality because somewhere along the line they are going to be sharing very personal information with you—about money and mortality. You must have good listening skills because prospects will be giving you important information, sometimes in informal settings.

Strategy

The cultivation process begins when you gather personal information to qualify the prospect and form a strategy for that person. The basic information you need includes philanthropic intent, values, family situation including children, assets, and financial and tax goals. You should also find out if the prospect is working with an attorney or a financial planner.

The strategy for your prospect must take into account family information: family obligations, including children or grandchildren; college plans; handicapped family members; elderly parents; and, possibly a family business. The strategy must also take into account other charities the prospect wants to support and the level of that support.

Education is an important element of the cultivation process. It is likely that the prospect is interested in the library and wants to hear about your needs. The donor's perspective on the library's needs is very important in his or her consideration of a gift. What might be perceived as a major need by a prospect might not be perceived as a need by the library. By educating prospects about the library, you lessen the likelihood of receiving a donation you do not want or need or that might end up as a maintenance cost to the library.

During the cultivation process, bring prospects into the library. Involve them in programs and invite them to events. Let them see the library, its strengths and weaknesses. The library is a tremendous community resource, but prospects only have the opportunity to appreciate that by coming into the library and experiencing that resource.

The cultivation process should include many opportunities to bring prospects into the library. For this reason, all library staff members should be on board with the development effort because they can play an important role in the process, from helping to identify prospects to cultivating them. In some cases, they might even help with the solicitation of prospects based on their relationship with them.

Reference librarians are often on the "front-lines" of the fund-raising development process because of their work with patrons. Their work at the reference desk, both in helping patrons and in identifying regular users, should be greatly valued. Reference librarians are also very aware of the library's fund-raising needs because of what they learn about patron needs and the library's ability to serve those needs. The participation and support of the reference staff are crucial to the success of any library development program.

Solicitation

Solicitation is the act of asking for the planned-gift donation. This might well be the most intimidating part of all for librarians in the fund-raising process. In planned giving, the ideal solicitation is about *how* the gift will be made, not *whether* the gift will be made.

The first step in the solicitation process is to decide who is the best person to make the solicitation. Perhaps a peer, a board member, a planned-giving donor, or a volunteer should ask. Perhaps the library director should ask. Most likely, the library director should team up with the peer, volunteer, or board member when meeting with the prospect to make the solicitation call.

Next consider others whom you should include. Are there others who should be involved in the solicitation? You might want to involve the donor's attorney or financial planner. Another option is to make the solicitation and offer to meet with the donor's financial advisor. It can work the other way around, with you meeting first with the financial planner or attorney and then making the solicitation to the prospect. Because a planned gift has elements of financial, tax, and estate planning, it is important to keep those advisors involved in the process.

Then the planned giving proposal is crucial. The proposal must include calculations of financial and tax benefits. Planned-giving software includes illustrations of calculations, and these are crucial to helping the donor understand the structure of the gift. Some software packages contain different illustrations for the donor and for the financial advisors, and that can be very beneficial as well.

The body of the proposal should be in prose form and should minimally include the program proposal, the plan for recognition, and the planned-giving calculations representing the mechanics of the donation. Be prepared to leave the proposal with the prospect, because usually the prospect will need to consider both the proposal and the mechanics. Remember, it need not be a long document, and it should be clear and to the point. See figures 4.1, 4.2, and 4.3.

Date

Mr. and Mrs. Donor
123 "A" Street
Anywhere, State

Dear Mr. and Mrs. Donor:

It is a pleasure to learn of your interest in supporting the Local Library. Your gift is especially appreciated as we work to build the endowment for the library's future. I'm enclosing some information about Local Library for you to review.

As we discussed, a charitable remainder annuity trust may be an excellent way to achieve your goals both for yourself and for the Library. You mentioned you would like to diversify your portfolio and increase your income. You are interested in a stable income not affected by the "ups and downs" of the market. Based on the information you gave me that you are 75 and 72, respectively, and that your income tax bracket is 39.6 percent, I am providing an illustration for a 6 percent charitable remainder annuity trust.

For example, if you irrevocably transfer $100,000 in property with a cost basis of $25,000 to an annuity trust that pays 6 percent of its initial value each year for your lifetimes, your benefits will include:

1. Charitable Income Tax Deduction of approximately $46,211. Note that deductions for this and other gifts of long-term appreciated property will be limited to 30 percent of your adjusted gross income. You may, if necessary, take unused deductions of this kind over the next five years, subject to the same 30 percent limitation.

2. Your designated income beneficiaries will receive fixed income in quarterly installments totaling $6,000 each year for life. This could result in as much as $61,608 in total after-tax income during your lifetimes.

3. Your entire gift property will be available for reinvestment, free of capital gains tax. If you were to sell and reinvest this property yourself, you would be taxed on $75,000 of capital gain.

4. Your estate may enjoy reduced probate costs and estate taxes.

5. Your gift will benefit from expert asset management provided by the same professionals who manage Local Library's endowment.

Most important, however, you will provide generous support to Local Library. As always, when considering a charitable gift, you should consult your tax advisors with regard to the most appropriate approach that will meet your individual needs. Thank you for your interest in Local Library. It is friends like you who help to create the Library's future. I look forward to talking with you about this gift plan or other gift opportunities with you.

Sincerely,

A. Staffperson

Figure 4.1   Sample Proposal Letter for Charitable Remainder Trust to the Library

Prepared for:
Mr. and Mrs. Donor

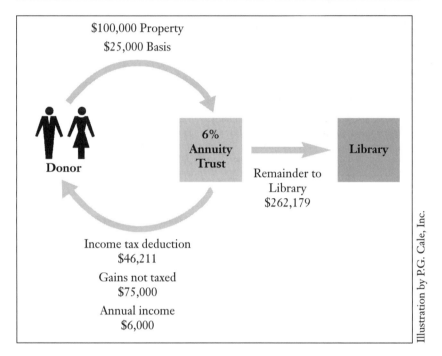

Benefits

Immediate

Income tax deduction of $46,211. May save up to $18,300. Pay no capital gains tax. May save up to $15,000.

Annual

Annual income of $6,000. Projected total after-tax income of $61,608 over 17 years.

Future

Library projected to receive $262,179 in 17 years. Reduced estate taxes and costs.

Figure 4.2   6 Percent Charitable Remainder Annuity Trust

Local Library

Prepared for:
Mr. and Mrs. Donor
January 20, 2000

Life Income Projections

Summary of Benefits

Assumptions

Projection begins in 2000 and runs for 17 years.

Measuring lives ages 75, 72.

Original principal is $100,000. Cost basis is 25%.

Donor income tax bracket is 39.6%, 20% for capital gains.

Beneficiary income tax bracket is 39.6%, 20% for capital gains.

	Charitable Annuity Trust 6%
Gross Principal	$ 100,000
Charitable Deduction	$ 46,211
Tax Savings	$ 18,300
Cost of Gift	$ 81,700
Income	6%
Capital Appreciation	4%
Total Before-Tax Benefit to Income Recipients	$ 102,000
Total After-Tax Benefit to Income Recipients	**$ 61,608**
Benefit to Library	**$262,179**
Total Benefit	**$323,787**

Prepared by: A. Staffperson   IRS Discount Rate is 7.4%

Note: This illustration is for educational purposes only and is merely intended to provide information based on certain assumptions. The donor or others should not interpret this information as legal, tax, or financial advice. Before entering into a planned or deferred giving arrangement, the donor should seek competent professional legal and tax opinion.

Figure 4.3 Summary of Benefits

Stewardship

Stewardship is more than just thanking the donor. Literally, to steward means to carry, and in the fund-raising sense, to steward means to carry the gift the donor has given you. The donor has given you something of great value, and it is up to you to take care of this gift.

Another way of thinking about successful stewardship is to take the Golden Rule and turn it on its axis: rather than "treat others the way *you* want to be treated," the rule for good stewardship is "treat your donors the way *they* want to be treated." Make sure you have a sense of the level and type of recognition that the donor wants: the hope is that you are able to accommodate your donor's desire. In any case, make sure that your actions are consistent with the donor's motivations.

Types of Recognition

It is suggested that you include a paragraph about recognition in any proposal you submit. For libraries, it is easy to promise bookplates or electronic recognition either in the public access catalog (PAC) or on a donor page on your library's Web page. During negotiations of the gift, you can explore other, more in-depth types of recognition, including—for large gifts—a press conference. One library has held press conferences in a public space in the building to announce its largest gifts; in all cases, it was a wonderful recognition opportunity that delighted the donors. It was also a great opportunity for library staff and faculty to gather and show their appreciation to the donor.

Who thanks the donor? In academic libraries, the dean, the university president, and the chair of your planned-giving advisory board should thank the donor. In a public library, the president of the board of trustees, the chair of the planned-giving advisory board, and the library director should thank the donor. There should always be an acknowledgment from the foundation receiving the property. It is a good idea to have policies on gift recognition that specify which signatures appear on gifts of various levels.

In addition to thanking the donor, there needs to be some public recognition of the gift. There are times when donors wish to remain anonymous, but often they understand that announcing the gift publicly educates the public to planned-giving opportunities. You should find out how your donor wishes to be recognized. Would she like a plaque? What kind of ceremony does he feel is appropriate? It is acceptable to tell the donor what you would like to do and ask for reactions and suggestions.

For some donations, bookplates and electronic recognition work well; for others, plaques are more appropriate. In other circumstances, planned gifts are honored with naming opportunities for rooms, wings, or buildings, depending on the size of the gift. Policies and procedures should be in place before the recognition issue comes up.

Does your library have a heritage or bequest society? Recognition can include induction into the society. Does your library have a newsletter or bulletin board? Photographs of the donor should be included in those. Recognition is important not only as a way of thanking the donor for the gift, but also of educating the public about the gift and planting the idea for other prospects.

Stewardship is also about maintaining the relationship with the donor. This is crucial if the gift is in a revocable form or a charitable remainder trust, in which the donor can change the remainder charity. In these cases, you must maintain the relationship so the donor is not inclined to change his or her mind about giving the gift to you after all. Maintaining the relationship can also lead to other gifts.

Invite the donor to lunch, to programs, to meet with other prospects and donors. Involve donors in the library and honor them for their generosity. Often, donors are capable of other donations; do not ignore the possibility that there may be more for your library from a particular donor. Keep the donor aware of other gift opportunities; the continued relationship can be even more valuable than you imagined.

Administration of Planned Gifts

Planned gifts are wonderful for the long-term needs of your library. However, administering and managing the gifts are involved and time-consuming. One might hope for the problem of how to administer all the planned gifts that pour into your library, but before that problem arises, it is preferable to have policies and procedures already in place.

You need gift acceptance policies. You may not want to accept every gift offered you for various reasons: the cost of maintaining the gift, environmental issues on gifts of property, or liability concerns for your library.

Gift acceptance policies should also include how to handle gifts of cash, securities (both closely held and publicly traded), real estate, life insurance, annuities, trusts, pooled income funds, and tangible personal property. For example: Will your library hold the stocks or sell them? Will your library pay appraisal costs for real estate or tangible personal property? Does your library want to "own" life insurance policies? Do you have the staff to administer trusts, annuities, and pooled income funds?

Other procedures have to do with investment policies. How should the funds be invested and how much of the income or principal should be used? Can endowment funds be used for emergency purposes?

Who is going to be responsible for the management of each gift, including substantiating gifts for the donor and preparing tax-reporting information? There is much to consider, and mismanaging gifts can cost your library greatly both in terms of credibility with donors and in fees later to correct mistakes.

Good planning can solve most of these potential problems. Working with a community foundation can also alleviate many of these concerns, as they will already have policies and procedures in place. Academic libraries should make sure the university foundation has policies and procedures in place.

Proper administration of the gift is key to good stewardship. This includes managing the gift (even if it is administered outside of your library), making sure IRS reporting requirements are met, and working with your foundation (or board) to make sure its members comply as well.

Regardless of size and support, make sure donors fill out tax form 8283. This is the donor's responsibility for any donation over $5,000. It is suggested that you include a copy of this form in correspondence with donors considering gifts over $5,000. Your library has the responsibility of filing form 8282 if the asset given is liquidated within two years of the donation. You must send a copy of this form to the donor. IRS forms can be downloaded from www.irs.gov/.

While the library should not be the gift manager, the librarian should be the donor manager. This is part of the stewardship process: to act as a liaison between the donor and the gift manager (bank, trust officer, or foundation) to make sure the donor is aware and satisfied with the management. The librarian must remember that regular communication, notes, invitations, and phone calls are part of stewarding donations and can lead to more donations as well.

5

Marketing Planned Giving

Getting the news out about your library's efforts to raise funds for the long-term viability of your library is what marketing is all about. In a pure sense, marketing your program is merely educating the public about planned-giving opportunities and benefits. There is a range of techniques to achieve this, some costly and some not.

Case Statements and Programs

The marketing of a planned-giving program begins with educating your director, the board of trustees, and the library staff. They all must understand the benefits and the limitations of a planned-giving program. Traditional wisdom on planned giving is that it takes five to seven years to produce results. Planned giving is a long-term process with future benefits. They need to support the program with a budget.

It is a universally acknowledged truth that librarians are used to small budgets. It is therefore assumed that you will probably have a shoestring budget to establish and develop a planned-giving program for your library. It is possible to have a planned-giving program on a modest budget. Regardless of size, there are some basic elements needed to establish and market a planned-giving program.

In addition to a budget to market the program, the director and board need to draft the statement of need. This statement, called the case statement, should be a collaborative project and should be an articulation of the library's long-term needs. Collaborating on the case statement puts everyone "on the same page" in terms of needs and expectations. In addition, the case statement is highly useful for prospects and can be incorporated into planned-giving proposals. A case statement should be concise and to the point. See figure 5.1 for a sample case statement.

From basic to deluxe, there are fundamental elements of marketing a planned-giving program. These include mailings, publications, advertising, seminars, events, and bequest societies. The adage "it takes money to make money" is generally true when it comes to marketing planned giving, and that is why a budget, of whatever size, is necessary.

Marketing means getting the news out about your program. You must let your prospects know that the library is seeking long-term support through planned gifts. You must also educate your prospects about planned giving. This can be accomplished through various marketing methods. The key elements of a planned-giving program are continuity, repetition, and perseverance.

Using various methods, you will need to continue to educate about planned gifts, repeat the message in various formats, and persevere for long-range success. In planned giving, you are dealing with money and mortality. Often, prospects take time to think about those issues. Chances are they will not make immediate decisions concerning a planned gift.

To whom are you marketing? You are marketing to your own board; to your directors; to your own faculty and staff (especially those with long careers in your library and no heirs); to regular and long-term donors; to professional advisors; and, of course, to your library patrons.

What are the most effective methods of marketing your planned-giving program? Remember the planned-giving marketing mantra: continuity, repetition, and perseverance.

Mailings

There are two types of mailings: indirect and direct. Indirect mailings include newsletter articles or ads in your other publications. In an academic environment, you can place planned-giving articles in other university-wide publications, including newsletters, alumni publications, annual reports, or messages from the president. Employee newsletters are another indirect mail opportunity.

Libraries and Learning Resources Fund

The University's Libraries and Learning Resources (LLR) face the enormous challenge of meeting the increasing information needs of students and faculty who need books, journals, online databases, music, and images to complete their assignments and research. Library faculty and staff help prepare graduates for a workplace where they will be required to find, evaluate, and use information at a very rapid pace. Library personnel also support university faculty who must have all forms of information at their fingertips to produce research and compete for grants.

The libraries at Bowling Green State University provide unique and innovative resources, technologies, and user-centered services. The collections in popular culture, the Great Lakes, and recorded music are among the largest in the United States and are consulted by researchers from around the world. Cutting-edge programs in the digitization of materials, the deployment of a First Year Experience Librarian, and distance training for area librarians make Bowling Green a leader in the library field. Financial support from donors has helped keep the Jerome Library facilities as beautiful and unique as its collections and services. Additional support will help move new programs forward and continue the libraries' reputation for excellence.

A gift to the Libraries and Learning Resources Development Fund can

- Build new group study rooms where students can perform research collaboratively;
- Provide students with laptop computers to facilitate their research anywhere in the building;
- Construct a new wing for the Jerome Library to house and protect the rare and precious materials needing special conditions of light, security, and temperature control;
- Provide new exhibit areas that can showcase not only the libraries' treasures but also those of the University as a whole for thousands of campus visitors each year;
- Help the Libraries purchase books, journals, and databases in support of new disciplines and new areas of emphasis.

Libraries and Learning Resources Development Fund
Office of Development
Bowling Green State University
Bowling Green, Ohio 43403
(419) 372-2424
Email: develop@bgnet.bgsu.edu

> No great university can exist without a great library. Our library is a place for everyone to study, perform research, and think. It also represents the university's investment in education's highest values: preserving the scholarship of the past, informing the scholarship of the present, and helping students and faculty create new scholarship for the future.

Linda Dobb is Dean of the Libraries and Learning Resources at BGSU.

Figure 5.1 Case Statement

Friends' organization literature is an excellent place to include indirect mailings about planned giving. If you have an annual giving program, you can easily incorporate information on planned gifts in the mailings and literature. Annual giving reply cards should include a line for prospects desiring information on making a bequest or a planned gift.

Direct mailings include brochures, year-end mailings, and bequest mailings. These direct mail pieces are specifically for planned giving. Timing is important. Fall is an excellent time to promote the tax benefits of planned giving. Prospects consider making charitable donations at year-end and, depending on their tax situation, may be more inclined to consider a larger donation then.

Winter and spring are good times to promote bequests. Many prospects travel during the winter, especially from the north to warmer southern climes. Some plan foreign travel. This travel planning season may be a good time for prospects to think about writing or updating their wills. Summer is generally not a good time to promote a planned-giving program: prospects are traveling or away at vacation homes. They are generally in the vacation mode and do not want to consider planned giving at that time.

Brochures

Brochures are an essential publication for any planned-giving program. A brochure is a great avenue for educating prospects about planned giving. Brochures may be mailed to targeted audiences or they may be handed out at seminars and events. You can also leave brochures with prospects after a cultivation call.

A brochure should include giving options. This should be kept as simple as possible so as not to overload the prospect with technical jargon. Short examples of each type of gift should be included. A brochure should also include information on the bequest society, including bequest language for wills. The most important element of a planned-giving brochure is the reply card requesting more information about planned gifts. Ideally, the request card should include a self-addressed, postage-paid return envelope. You want to make it as easy as possible for the prospect to follow through. A name and phone number should also be included in the brochure. In some cases, you can insert your business card instead.

If you intend to send the brochure to a targeted audience, you will need to send it with a cover letter. The letter should make the case for long-term support of your library; it should be short and to the point.

Newsletters

Planned-giving newsletters are ideal. They can highlight different aspects of planned giving, including estate planning, tax planning, and financial planning. They can also highlight various planned-giving vehicles. In addition, newsletters should include articles about donors and their gifts, and, whenever possible, photographs of the donor or the gift. Newsletters should also include an honor roll of planned-giving donors.

Like brochures, newsletters should include a reply card requesting further information and a name and number for prospects to contact. Unlike brochures, newsletters should be published on a regular basis, three or four times a year. If you do not have a budget for regular publication of newsletters, you can place an article on planned giving in other newsletters; these also should appear on a regular and ongoing basis. If you cannot supply a reply card in those other publications, always include a name and phone number for donors to contact.

A variation of the piggyback approach to planned-giving articles is the buckslip. Buckslips are very short and simple pieces of information about planned giving that are included in other mailings. The purpose of the buckslip is to allow donors to request more information about planned gifts.

Advertising

Another specific marketing method is advertising. Ads can be created that include short testimonials to educate prospects about planned-giving options. They can also include photographs of donors. The California Foundation ran a series of ads in the *Wall Street Journal* that included photographs of California legacies, including the Griffith Observatory in Los Angeles and Yosemite Falls. The ads were very powerful because of the photographs. There was little prose, but contact information was given for further information.

Advertising in the *Wall Street Journal* may be a stretch for most libraries. However, consider some strategic sites for your ad: perhaps your local paper, the alumni magazine, the Friends' newsletter, donor publications, or, in the university setting, the extended education publication is an effective advertising site. After all, the audience for extended education includes retirees.

Advertisements are teasers. Because of space limitations, you usually cannot use ads to educate your prospects. You need to create an item that catches their attention and compels them to request further information. For that reason, a check-off box or response form is essential. To follow up on these requests, send out a standard outline of planned-giving options and then follow up with a personal phone call.

Budget Constraints

In the real world all these marketing tools cost money. Brochures and newsletters can be very expensive to produce. There are many options to consider, depending on your budget.

One option is for you to create your own publications. Costs include your time to write, design, and produce these items. If design is not your forte, you can have a graphic artist help you. Then you must pay for printing costs. Consider as well the mailing costs of sending a brochure or regular newsletters.

Another option is to purchase prepared newsletters and brochures from a professional planned-giving marketing company. There are many to choose from, including the Stelter Company, Pentera, Robert F. Sharpe, and R. and R. Newkirk. A comprehensive list of marketing companies can be found in the Planned Giving Resources appendix. These companies offer a range of standard marketing materials that can be personalized for your organization. Prices vary depending on your needs.

Volunteers

Another option is to look to your Friends and volunteers. Is there a graphic artist among them who would be willing to help design your publications at a reduced rate? Do you have any printers who might help the library? Do any of your Friends or volunteers know someone who might help at a reduced cost? Remember that your publications do not need to be glitzy to be effective. They need to convey the essential information that your library is looking for planned gifts for long-term goals, a basic explanation of planned giving, and a contact for prospects to receive additional information.

Events and Seminars

Seminars and events can be immeasurably helpful in marketing your planned-giving programs. An event for professionals in your community can be a highly effective way of letting them know that your library is in the planned-giving business. In turn, they can guide clients or let clients know about this giving opportunity.

Professionals to include in these events are estate-planning attorneys, accountants, trust officers, life insurance professionals, real estate brokers, and financial planners. Ostensibly the event is to offer them information on charitable giving, but the other purpose is to let them know that your library is looking for planned gifts. If possible, you should offer continuing education credit for the professionals because it is difficult for them to take billable hours off to attend a program and not get anything in return.

Another very effective event is the wills seminar for your prospects. Ask an estate-planning attorney to speak on the importance of proper will preparation including how to make charitable gifts through a will. It is astonishing that nearly 80 percent of people die without a will. Attendees at these events are self-identified planned-giving prospects and you should follow up with them after the event.

Bequests

Most planned gifts come through bequests. This is because most prospects believe they need their assets while they are alive. Marketing a bequest program is a great beginning to a larger planned-giving program. It is simple and much less expensive.

The simplest and most effective marketing tool is suggesting bequests in every publication. Let your prospects know how bequests can benefit your library and that your library is actively looking for bequests. You can do this through small ads or newsletter articles placed in various publications. You can include bequest information on annual giving materials or simply include a check-box requesting information on pledge cards or in newsletters.

Include bequest language in publications. At the same time, always publish your library's legal name and address. If you have already received bequests, include a photograph or donor profile.

Create a bequest society with the purpose of publicly recognizing donors for their gifts. Bequest societies are also highly useful in the stewardship of a donation by recognizing the donor publicly and honoring him or her both in print and at a bequest society event.

Bequest societies are also very effective means for educating other donors. Bequest society publications should be sent to all your planned-giving prospects, not just to society members. Use the society's publications and events to communicate the benefits of planned giving both to donors and to your library.

The essential elements of a bequest society are your name, an inclusion policy, and your recognition methods. You will need an honor roll format as well as an induction ceremony. An annual event is very effective for inducting new members and honoring all members of the bequest society.

The basic elements of marketing a planned-giving program include effectively getting information to prospects that your library is seeking long-term support through planned gifts, including bequests; following up on all inquiries about planned giving, including simple but thorough information on the various planned-giving vehicles; and, good stewardship for donors who come through. Bequest societies are the most effective way to honor and recognize your donors. Marketing is essential to educate your prospects and the public.

6

Advisory Boards

The purpose of any fund-raising development board can be distilled as to "give time, treasure, and wisdom" or, in a more vulgarized version, "give, get, or get out of the way." The loftier version is especially true for a planned-giving advisory board, because it is the *wisdom* of the board members that will reap the greatest rewards for your library. As Hannah Gray has said, "Boards exist . . . for the sustenance of a mission, for the perpetuation of the institution in which [the board] is embodied over time."[1]

For development advisory boards in general, as well as for boards of trustees, it is expected that members make a financial contribution to your institution. If they are not able to give at a substantial level, they should be able to provide access, and hopefully help get donations at a high level, through their connections.

Rule and Makeup of Advisory Boards

The emphasis on giving is not as crucial for a planned-giving advisory board as it is for other development advisory boards. In fact, it is important not to load your board with only "rich widows with no heirs" and expect that they all will make planned gifts to your library. Rather, it is more important to load your board with professional advisors and members of the community who can lead you to rich widows with no heirs— or other planned-giving prospects. Of course it would be ideal if some of your board members made a planned gift in the course of their tenure on the board, but because of the professional makeup of the board, including the range in age of the members, that is unlikely to happen.

For a really effective planned-giving advisory board, the "wisdom" element is crucial and should be at least as highly valued in your selection of members as the "time" and "treasure."

Regardless of the size of your planned-giving budget, you will need to involve volunteers. The advisory board is the perfect place for volunteers to help you be successful in your planned-giving efforts. The most effective role of your advisory board is to help you implement your planned-giving program by giving professional advice, identifying prospects, and perhaps soliciting donations. You will need to involve a range of volunteers who can provide wisdom (professional advice and knowledge of prospects in the community), their time on a regular basis, and ideally, treasure—meaning a number of members who are capable and inclined to make a planned gift.

The professionals you will want on your advisory board include estate-planning attorneys, certified public accountants, insurance professionals, including chartered life underwriters, certified financial planners, trust officers, stockbrokers, and real estate professionals.

Identifying Board Members

Where to Find Them

Potential advisors for your board can be found in professional organizations in your community. Either visit or join the local chapter of the National Committee on Planned Giving (NCPG) to network with members of the allied professions. Local planned-giving councils are comprised of estate planning attorneys, life insurance professionals, accountants, trust officers, and, in some cases, real estate professionals. The councils usually have other planned-giving officers as members as well.

Joining the organization presents a great opportunity to let the professional community know that your library is starting a planned-giving program. You will meet the professionals in your community who are involved in planned giving and have the ability to help your program. Members of the local planned-giving councils are excellent prospects for advisory board members for your program.

The councils are also highly beneficial for their educational programs. Many hold regular monthly meetings on planned-giving topics, as well as annual conferences. If your local chapter does not have an annual conference, contact NCPG to find out where the regional conference will be held. The conferences are excellent for learning about planned-giving topics and for networking with allied professionals and other planned-giving directors, as well as for finding out about planned-giving support (software, journals, marketing, and so on).

Other professional organizations to visit or join include an estate planning council and the local chapter of the National Society of Fund Raising Executives. Both offer great opportunities for networking and education as well as fertile ground for finding potential advisors to help your program.

The local estate planning councils are comprised of estate-planning attorneys, accountants, life insurance professionals, and possibly other planned-giving officers. This council, unlike the planned-giving councils, consists of professionals involved in estate planning for clients; planned giving, although always an option for a client, is not the focus. However, most members of the estate planning council are aware of planned giving and will have knowledge about it. They may even be eager to learn more about planned giving and will view the opportunity of serving on your advisory board as a practical method of learning more.

Your local chapter of the National Society of Fund Raising Executives is made up of professionals involved in fund-raising, including annual giving, major gifts, and planned giving for nonprofits and foundations. Public relations professionals involved with nonprofits also attend. NSFRE is an excellent organization for learning more about fund-raising overall, and often it offers educational programs that include planned giving.

Who Are Potential Advisors?

Estate planning attorneys work with clients to prepare their estate plans. Often they ask about their client's charitable giving and incorporate that into the estate plans. By including estate-planning attorneys, you have the opportunity to let them know that the library is seeking long-term support. They, in turn, can suggest the library as a charitable option to their clients in their estate planning. Often estate-planning attorneys are knowledgeable about planned-giving options and can be an excellent source of information for you. Estate-planning attorneys can help prepare trust documents as well.

Accountants provide beneficial information on tax and financial planning. Certified public accountants (CPAs) often have the best financial picture of a prospect and will want to find ways to preserve and grow a client's assets. Accountants also have a foundation in tax planning and compliance with tax rules. They can be helpful in responding to tax-related issues that might arise in the course of structuring a planned gift.

Life insurance professionals, some of whom are chartered life underwriters (CLUs), work with clients in the area of estate planning. Their area of expertise is especially helpful in wealth replacement, since that includes life insurance. Often life insurance professionals are very supportive of planned gifts because of the insurance component in structuring such gifts.

Financial planners are involved in the financial aspect of estate planning. There is a wide range of financial planners, including Certified Financial Planners (CFPs), Chartered Financial Planners (ChFPs), and financial planners who specialize in life insurance or stock portfolio management. They encompass a diverse group of professionals who often are supportive of planned giving because of the opportunities for financial and tax planning it provides for their clients.

Trust officers often have long relationships with donors based on the preservation and transfer of the donor's wealth. Trust officers can also provide support for planned-giving trust arrangements.

Stockbrokers can be helpful on the advisory board since they work with clients on the preservation and growth of assets. They are also involved in the management of wealth.

In communities where land is a major asset, it is a good idea to include *real estate professionals* on the advisory board. Real estate professionals can help identify planned-giving prospects as well as help structure a planned gift involving real estate. Often land used as an asset needs to be sold. Real estate brokers see the potential of commissions in structuring planned gifts.

All these professionals have influence over potential donors about the benefits of charitable giving. They work with clients on a daily basis facing issues of wealth preservation, growth, and transfer. Planned giving provides many benefits for their clients.

Benefits of Advisors

These professionals can give you valuable advice. As a librarian, you cannot be expected to be knowledgeable about all these allied professions. The board members can be immeasurably helpful in providing you with information and giving you advice. This is the crucial role of the advisory board: to advise.

The advisors can also provide expertise for seminars. Generally, the professional will want to help in this way since the seminar audience may well contain potential clients. Giving seminars is a marketing tool for many of these professionals, and they will be inclined to help the library by presenting at a seminar.

Offering seminars is part of the marketing function in a planned-giving program. However, it is desirable to have advisory board members who are willing to present at the seminars. The two most popular seminars are Wills and Estate Planning, which an attorney should give; and Financial and Tax Planning, which either an accountant or a financial planner should give.

If you have many women prospects, a seminar on financial planning for women will be popular. It would be helpful to have women professionals give these seminars.

Some of your advisors may already offer seminars as part of their own marketing efforts and would be willing to invite your prospects to attend. Consider an arrangement of co-sponsorship for seminars, with some of your advisors collaborating on an event for your prospects.

Certainly there is great potential for finding planned-giving prospects with the help of the professional advisors. They can direct clients. They can also become donors themselves. The professional advisors can also be highly effective in educating your director or trustees by clarifying concepts (and perhaps requesting a larger planned-giving budget). In some cases, the professional advisors may be willing to help present proposals to prospects. A planned gift may present a professional opportunity for them as well.

Benefits to Advisors

Once you have identified professional advisors who can offer the greatest benefit to your program, you need to consider why these busy professionals would want to take time from billable hours to volunteer for the library.

Professionals will want to help when they recognize the library's importance in the community. Are they patrons? Did they grow up in the community and use the library when they were younger? Have they seen a decline in service due to budget constraints and want to do something to help? Look to your patron base for potential advisors.

Many professionals feel good about doing good. They know that they will get personal satisfaction from helping the library. Often they recognize the importance and satisfaction of having a balance of work and volunteerism.

Some professionals may also enjoy the status of serving on the advisory board of the library. They might understand the personal and professional benefits of networking with the other professionals serving on the board. It would be helpful to understand what motivates your volunteers, just as it is important to understand the motivation of your donors. By understanding motivation, you can begin to maximize benefits.

Role of the Board

The role of an advisory board is to support your organization. This can be achieved through the giving of advice, the sharing of information, the influencing of clients and donors, and the providing of professional credibility to your program. Board members must all appreciate the benefits of planned giving, especially in regard to the library.

If you are establishing a planned-giving program, the advisory board must be instrumental in developing the policies and procedures for the program. This includes policies regarding types of gifts and the ways gifts should be administered. Board members should also provide direction on financial matters including investment policies.

You need to keep in mind that these professionals are volunteers for your library, but in their other lives, they depend on billable work. Even so, be assertive in asking the professionals to do work for the library. This could be asking an attorney to draft a document or an accountant to provide tax information. If they cannot provide the work pro bono, perhaps they will offer discounts on commissions.

Your professional advisors should also be chosen for their influence in the community. This lends credibility to your program, but it also helps in their ability to identify prospects. In addition, it is helpful when they volunteer to solicit planned gifts that they are well regarded by potential donors.

A working board offers the greatest potential for success of your planned-giving program. It is not enough to just form the board; you must maximize its collective expertise.

The National Center for Nonprofit Boards (http://www.NCNB. org/) in Washington, D.C., has information and training materials on board development.

Managing the Board

After forming the board, it is important to let it go. It is imperative for the board to feel ownership of its mission. The chair of the board should run the meetings and be willing to work collaboratively with you on setting the agenda. Other than that, your role becomes more of a manager of the board than the leader. You must facilitate the running of the board but not appear to be in control of it.

There's no question that managing a board takes time and effort. This includes recruiting new members in collaboration with existing members and your library director. You will need to make sure that new board members are oriented not only to the board but to the library. You must also manage regular and ongoing communication with board members between meetings, and follow up on activities requested by the board between meetings. Organizing the board meetings is crucial, including sending announcements, agendas, and parking passes in advance of the meetings. If lunch is to be served, you need to make sure those arrangements are in place.

In addition to managing the board, never forget your role in developing planned gifts. You must also manage the cultivation of board members. Much of the knowledge building crucial for donors deciding to make a gift will come through the process of serving on the board; however, you will still need to cultivate these board members as donors. Planned-giving decisions often take a long time to blossom, but in the meantime, keep these donors in mind for annual gifts or major, outright gifts. In addition, as manager of the board, you will need to be responsible for recording and recognizing gifts.

Putting Your Board to Work

The biggest favor you can do for your board members is to put them to work. Give them a plan with objectives. Make sure they understand from the beginning that the board is going to be a working committee. Goals should include

Establishing policies and procedures

Identifying prospects

Advising on planned gifts

In some cases, soliciting gifts

The advisory board should meet regularly. Depending on the needs of the program, the board might meet frequently too, but regularly is more important. Choose a regular time—perhaps at noon on the third Thursday of every month—so that members can plan ahead and depend on the consistency. It will also save you from the nightmare of trying to set up a convenient meeting time for ten or twelve busy professionals.

Make the meeting time as convenient as possible. For example, hold a lunch meeting and provide box lunches for members. Try to choose the most convenient location for all. Whenever possible, provide parking permits as well, so valuable time isn't lost trying to find parking. Send meeting reminders by fax, e-mail, or regular mail at least a week in advance. The reminder should also include an agenda for the upcoming meeting.

The agenda should be consistent with perhaps a variation on a regular basis. Perhaps once a quarter or twice a year, you can vary the agenda by inviting a guest presenter. It might be helpful to arrange to have the board meet library department heads or visit different areas of the library to learn more about the resources the library provides. If you have an electronic classroom, take the board to the classroom for a demonstration. Do not assume that your board members are familiar with all the resources of the library. Show them. Varying the agenda gives you the opportunity to educate your board in a nonthreatening manner.

Solicit feedback from board members. Are they doing what they thought they would be doing? Do they have suggestions for improving the board effort? Soliciting feedback and advice should be done individually and not at a meeting of the whole. Plan to check in with each board member on a one-to-one basis at least once during the year.

Stewardship

The success of your board also depends on your willingness to cultivate and steward the board. Make it as easy as possible for the board to run effectively and to feel useful.

Recognize your board members. Hold an annual recognition event for them. Thank them and honor them for their support. Recognize retiring members and welcome new members. Invite former members. The event should be social, but it should also include an update or list of achievements of the year. The social event should be held in a location different from that of the regular board meetings and should be livelier and more attractive. You might consider inviting spouses, depending on your budget.

For an academic library, invite the university president. For a public library, invite members of your board of trustees so they can thank your board members for their work. This gives the board members an opportunity to feel appreciated by the top.

Cultivation and stewardship take place on many levels in the realm of planned giving. Besides the cultivation of donors, you must remember to cultivate your volunteers. Stewardship of volunteers is as important as stewardship of donors. They are both giving something of great value and need to be recognized for that gift.

The advisory board is crucial to having a successful program, from establishing policies and procedures to getting advice, identifying donors, and helping solicit gifts. Make sure your board knows how grateful you are for their time, effort, and wisdom.

Planned-giving advisory boards are most successful when the "time, treasure, and wisdom" mantra is reordered as "wisdom, time, and possibly treasure." Choose your members for their knowledge, connections in the community, and willingness to work. Ideally, your board will be successful in bringing in some gifts, and this in turn will inspire gifts of their own.

Note

1. William G. Bowen, *Inside the Boardroom: Governance by Directors and Trustees* (New York: J. Wiley, 1994).

Planned-Giving Resources

PLANNED-GIVING CONSULTING AND MARKETING RESOURCES

John Brown Limited, Inc.
Box 296 46 Grove Street
Peterborough, NH 03458-0296
603-924-3834

Converse & Associates
6363 Poplar Avenue
Memphis, TN 38119
901-684-1181

Legacies
Southwest Office:
Matthew D. Lehrer
(520) 745-0498
East Coast Office:
David H. Belkin
(301) 986-0352
plannedgift@earthlink.net
www.plannedgift.net

R&R Newkirk Company
8695 S. Archer Avenue, #10
Willow Springs, IL 60480
800-342-2375

Pentera, Inc.
8650 Commerce Park Place, Suite G
Indianapolis, IN 46268
317-875-0910

Robert F. Sharpe & Company
5050 Poplar Avenue
Memphis, TN 38157
800-238-3253

Sinclair, Townes & Company
1750 Candler Building
127 Peachtree Street, NE
Atlanta, GA 30303
404-688-4047

Winton C. Smith Jr.
2670 Union Ext., Suite 1200
Memphis, TN 38112
800-727-1040

Stelter Company
11159 Aurora Avenue
Des Moines, IA 50322
800-331-6881

PLANNED GIVING SOFTWARE

Beneview
View Plan
P.O. Box 80788
San Diego, CA 92138-7088
800-826-2127

Brentmark
120 University Park Drive, Suite 280
Winter Park, FL 32792-4427
800-879-6665

Charitable Quick Plan
Kettley Publishing
800-777-3162

The Charitable Scenario
PhilanthroTec, Inc.
10800 Independence Pointe Pwky.,
    Suite F
Matthews, NC 28105
800-332-7832

Crescendo Software
Comdel, Inc.
1601 Carmen Drive
Camarillo, CA 93010
800-858-9154

DASCO II
Donor Automation, Inc.
912 New York Street, Suite B
Redlands, CA 92374
909-793-1230

DB Cultivator
Oaktree Systems
4462 Middle Country Road
Calverton, NY 11933
800-726-8163

Denari 4.3 for Windows
Synergy Development Systems, Inc.
20423 State Road 7
Boca Raton, FL 33498
800-352-0312

Donor II for Windows
Systems Support Service
8848-B Red Oak Boulevard
Charlotte, NC 28217-5518
800-548-6708

Enterprise, Access
Access International
432 Columbia Street
Cambridge, MA 02141
617-494-0066

Friars
Balassaitis Development Systems
101 Hampshire Court
Deptford, NJ 08096-4214
609-228-1110

Fund Accounting/Donor Records
Executive Data Systems, Inc.
1640 Powers Ferry Road
Building 27
Marietta, GA 30067
770-955-3374

Fund Accounting Systems
McAllister Associates, Inc.
274 Main Street
Reading, MA 01867
617-942-0700

Fundware
American Fundware, Inc.
1385 South Colorado Boulevard,
    Suite 400
Denver, CO 80222
800-551-4458

Gift Planning Assistant II
Brennan Analytical
P.O. Box 1538
Wall, NJ 07719
908-681-2554

**IMIS Association/Nonprofit
    Software**
Advanced Solutions International
3309 Duke Street
Alexandria, VA 22314
800-727-8682

Member Donor System
McAllister Associates, Inc.
274 Main Street
Reading, MA 01867
617-942-0700

Micromailer
MIRUS
730 East Park Boulevard, Suite 104
Plano, TX 75074
800-826-4787

Millennium
JSI FundRaising Systems, Inc.
4732 Longhill Road, Suite 2201
Williamsburg, VA 23188
800-574-5772

**MIP Nonprofit Series for
    Windows**
Micro Information Products, Inc.
505 East Huntland Drive, Suite 340
Austin, TX 78752
800-647-3863

Paradigm
JSI FundRaising Systems, Inc.
44 Farnsworth Street
Boston, MA 02210-1211
800-521-0132

PG Calc
PG Calc, Inc.
129 Mount Auburn Street
Cambridge, MA 02138
617-497-4970

Pledgemaker
SofTrek
606 N. French Road
Amherst, NY 14228
716-691-1141

Riss/Friss Donor Development
Advantage Solution, Inc.
350 S. Schmale Road
Carol Stream, IL 60188-2789
630-668-1598

Summit
University Systems Technology, Inc.
137 Lynn Avenue, Suite 208
Ames, IA 50014
515-296-2606

Symantec
Symantec Corporation
10201 Torre Avenue
Cupertino, CA 95104
800-441-7234

An online source for planned giving
    software is

http://www.deathandtaxes.com/
    Links/software.htm

PERIODICALS

Advancing Philanthropy
Published quarterly by the National
    Society of Fund Raising
    Executives (NSFRE)
1101 King Street, Suite 700
Alexandria, VA 22314
703-684-0410

Charitable Gift Planning News
Published monthly by Jerry J.
    McCoy and Terry L. Simmons
P.O. Box 214373
Dallas, TX 75221-4373
972-386-8975

Chronicle of Philanthropy
Published biweekly by the
Chronicle of Higher
Education, Inc.
1255 23rd Street, N.W.
Washington, DC 20037
202-466-1200

Currents
Published monthly by the Council
for Advancement and Support
of Education
11 Dupont Circle, Suite 400
Washington, DC 20036
202-328-5900

Fund Raising Management
Published monthly by Hoke
Communications, Inc.
224 Seventh Street
Garden City, NY 11530
516-746-6700

Giving USA Update
Published quarterly by the
American Association of Fund-
Raising Counsel Trust for
Philanthropy
25 W. 43rd Street, Suite 820
New York, NY 10036
212-354-5799

Journal of Gift Planning
Published quarterly by the National
Committee on Planned Giving
233 McCrea, Suite 400
Indianapolis, Indiana 46225
317-269-6274

*New Directions for Philanthropic
Fundraising*
Published quarterly by Jossey-Bass
Inc., Indiana University, Center
on Philanthropy
350 Sansome Street, 5th Floor
San Francisco, CA 94104
888-378-2537

NonProfit Times
Published monthly by Davis
Information Group
240 Cedar Knolls Road, Suite 318
Cedar Knolls, NJ 07927-1621
201-734-1700

Philanthropic Studies Index
Published three times a year by
Indiana University Press, Indiana
University, Center on
Philanthropy
601 N. Morton Street
Bloomington, IN 47404
800-842-6796

Philanthropic Trends Digest
Published bimonthly by Douglas M.
Lawson Associates, Inc.
545 Madison Avenue
New York, NY 10022
212-759-5660

Planned Giving Today
Published monthly by G. Roger
Schoenhals
100 Second Avenue South,
Suite 180
Edmonds, WA 98020
425-744-3837

Trusts and Estates
Published monthly by Intertec
  Publishing Corp.
6151 Powers Ferry Road, N.W.
Atlanta, GA 30339-2941
770-955-2500

Women's Philanthropy
Published quarterly by the National
  Network on Women as
  Philanthropists
1300 Linden Drive
Madison, WI 53706-1575
608-262-1962

INTERNET RESOURCES
GIFT-PL
GIFT-PL is an electronic discussion
  list dedicated to planned-giving
  information, issues, and
  questions. You can subscribe
  by sending an e-mail message
  to: listserv@iupui.edu

Leave the subject line blank. In the
body of the message, type: subscribe
gift-pl your name.

LIBDEV
LIBDEV is the electronic discussion
  list for ALADN, the national
  organization of academic library
  development professionals
  (Academic Library Advancement
  and Development Network). You
  can subscribe by sending an e-
  mail message to: libdev@listserv.
  arizona.edu

Leave the subject line blank. In the
body of the message, type: subscribe
LIBDEV your name.

LAMA Fundraising
FRFDS-L is a moderated discussion
  list that focuses on issues pertain-
  ing to fund-raising and resource
  development for libraries. To
  subscribe, send an e-mail
  message to: Listproc@ala.org

Leave the subject line blank or type
"subscribe" if your system requires a
subject. Put as the only line in the
body of the message: subscribe
FRFDS-L YourFirstName
YourLastName

CharitySoft
CharitySoft is an international
  discussion list covering the
  Internet and charities and
  software and charities. It is
  hosted by the American
  Philanthropy Review. To
  subscribe, send an e-mail
  message to Listserv@Charity
  Channel.com

In the body of the message type:
SUBSCRIBE CHARITYSOFT
Your FirstName Your LastName
or point your browser to http://
CharityChannel.com/Forums and
select "Subscribe, Unsubscribe, or
Modify Subscription Options" link
in the "CharitySoft" section.

PLANNED-GIVING INFORMATION
http://www.actec.org
American College of Trust and
  Estate Counsel

http://www.pgresources.com/
sumrates/html
American Council on Gift Annuities
(ACGA) rates and other helpful
information

http://www.philanthropy-
review.com
American Philanthropy Review

http://philanthropy-review.com/
Consultants Registry Online

http://philanthropy-review.
com/forums/
CharityChannel's Internet
discussion lists and Web-based
forums hosted by American
Philanthropy Review

http://CharityChannel.com
The Internet discussion forums of
American Philanthropy Review

http://members.aol.com/crtrust/
CRT.html
Charitable Trust Planning, created
by Vaughn Henry and Associates

http://philanthropy.com
The Chronicle of Philanthropy

http://www.cof.org
Foundation News and Commentary,
a bimonthly magazine of the
Council on Foundations

http://www.tcop.org
Indiana University Center on
Philanthropy

http://www.nonprofits.org
Internet Nonprofit Center

http://www.ncpg.org
National Committee on Planned
Giving

http://www.nptimes.com
NonProfit Times, a monthly
newsletter for nonprofits

http://philanthropy-journal.org
Philanthropy Journal Online

http://www.pj.org/plhome/
pllistserv
Philanthropy Journal online site for
discussion lists

http://fdcenter.org
Philanthropy News Digest,
published by the Foundation
Center

http://www.plannedgiving.com
Suggested Policies and Procedures
plus Marketing Concepts, Tax
Issues, published by T. Joseph
McKay, 2011 Oakhurst Parkway,
Sugar Land, TX 77479

http://www.guidestar.org
Searchable directory of nonprofit
organizations

http://www.goingv.com/pgdc/
Planned Giving Design Center

http://www.taxwisegiving.com
Taxwise Giving and Philanthropy
Tax Institute, 13 Arcadia Road,
Old Greenwich, CT 06870

PROFESSIONAL ASSOCIATIONS

American Library Association
Fund Raising and Financial
  Development Section
50 East Huron Street
Chicago, IL 60611
1-800-545-2433
http://www.ala.org/lama/

**Council for Advancement and
  Support of Education (CASE)**
11 Dupont Circle, N.W., Suite 400
Washington, DC 20036
202-328-5900
www.case.org

Council on Foundations
1828 L. Street, N.W., Suite 300
Washington, DC 20036
202-466-6512
www.cof.org

**National Committee on Planned
  Giving (NCPG)**
233 McCrea Street, Suite 400
Indianapolis, IN 46225
317-269-6274
www.ncpg.org

**National Society of Fund Raising
  Executives (NSFRE)**
1101 King Street, Suite 700
Alexandria, VA 22314
703-684-0410
www.nsfre.org

Women and Philanthropy
1015 18th Street, N.W.
Washington, DC 20036
www.womenphil.org

Women's Philanthropy Institute
6314 Odana Road, Suite 1
Madison, WI 53719-1141
www.women-philanthropy.org

GLOSSARY

Adjusted gross income (AGI)   A federal tax term for gross income minus certain deductions but before exemptions and itemized deductions (including the charitable deduction) are subtracted to determine taxable income.

Annual exclusion   Each $10,000 gift given by one individual to another is excluded from federal gift taxes.

Annuitant   An individual or entity who receives an annuity.

Annuity   Payment made periodically and based on life expectancy. An annuity is usually a fixed amount, paid at least annually, during lifetime.

Annuity trust   Another name for a charitable remainder annuity trust in which the trust payment is fixed and is a percentage of the initial value of the trust assets. The term can also refer to a charitable lead annuity trust.

Applicable federal rate (AFR)   This can also be called the charitable midterm federal rate (CMFR). A percentage rate, published monthly by the IRS, is used to calculate charitable deductions for charitable remainder trusts, pooled income funds, charitable gift annuities, and charitable lead trusts. The rate is based on 120 percent of the average market yield of U.S. obligations and provides an estimate of the fund's earning potential.

Appraisal   A determination of the value of an asset by a qualified appraiser.

Appreciated property   Property or items that have gone up in value since they were purchased.

Appreciation   The increased value of an asset from the time it was purchased to its current value.

Bargain sale   When property is sold to a charity for less than its appraised fair market value.

Basis The original cost of an asset, minus depreciation (lowering of value) allowed or allowable as a tax deduction, plus improvements. The basis portion of an asset is not taxed when it is sold.

Bear market A cycle in the stock market in which the value of stocks declines.

Beneficiary The individual named to receive assets, either from a life insurance policy, a will or trust, or a pension plan.

Bequest Gift made through a will.

Big board Another name for the New York Stock Exchange.

Bull market A cycle in the stock market in which the value of stocks continues to increase.

C corporation An ordinary corporation in which the corporation's income is taxed even though the income is distributed to shareholders who pay income tax on the income. In a sense, a C corporation is taxed twice.

Capital asset An investment asset or a business asset, but not inventory of a business.

Capital gain The appreciation in an asset.

Capital gain property Property that has increased in value and has been held for one year or longer.

Capital gain tax The tax paid on the increase in value of an asset when the asset is sold.

Carry over Also called a "carry forward." When a donor gives an asset, he or she can carry over the tax benefit of the gift for up to five years following the tax year that the gift was made.

Charitable gift annuity A contract between a donor and a charity whereby the donor gives an asset and, in return, the charity agrees to pay an annuity to the donor.

Charitable lead annuity trust A trust arrangement that pays a fixed amount annually to a charity or charities over a set number of years. At the end of the trust term, the assets revert to noncharitable beneficiaries.

Charitable lead unitrust Similar to the charitable lead annuity trust, except that the amount paid out to the charity is not fixed, but rather a percentage of the value of the asset, as revalued annually.

Charitable remainder annuity trust   A trust arrangement whereby a donor irrevocably transfers assets to a trust; the trust pays out a fixed amount at least annually to the donor or recipients named by the donor based on the initial value of the asset when the trust is established. At the end of the trust, or the death of the beneficiaries, the remainder in the trust is transferred to a charity or charities designated by the donor. Also called a CRAT.

Charitable remainder trust   Also called a CRT. The trust arrangement can either be a charitable remainder annuity trust or a charitable remainder unitrust.

Charitable remainder unitrust   A trust arrangement whereby a donor makes an irrevocable transfer of asset to a trust; the trust pays out a variable dollar amount at least annually, based on a set percentage of the value of the trust's assets as revalued annually. At the end of the trust, or the death of the beneficiaries, the remainder in the trust is transferred to a charity or charities designated by the donor. Also called a CRUT.

Charitable trust   A trust arrangement whereby either trust income or the remainder funds are designated to charities.

Codicil   An amendment to a will, usually to make minor changes.

Common stock   Securities that represent ownership shares in a corporation and which sometimes reward shareholders with dividends and capital appreciation.

Community property   Property acquired during a marriage, and each spouse is treated as owning equal shares. This means that neither spouse can dispose of more than half by will.

Corporation   An association of individuals created to limit their liabilities to assets that they have invested in a business or nonprofit arrangement. A corporation must be registered and operated according to state laws.

Corpus   The body of a trust referring to the principal amount in the trust and not the income.

Crummey power   This gives beneficiaries the power to make limited withdrawals from an irrevocable trust to obtain an annual gift tax exclusion of up to $10,000 for gifts to the trust. Generally, beneficiaries do not make the withdrawals, but they must have the option in order for the trust to qualify for the annual exclusion.

This reduces the gift tax cost of transferring enough cash to the trust to pay life insurance premiums (for an irrevocable life insurance trust).

Custodian The individual appointed to hold property for a minor under the Uniform Gifts to Minors Act or Uniform Transfers to Minors Act.

Deferred charitable gift annuity A charitable gift annuity in which the payments to the donor are deferred by at least one year.

Deferred giving Sometimes used interchangeably with planned giving, but is actually only a part of planned giving. Deferred giving occurs when a charity is required to wait at least a year to use a gift.

Devise A testamentary gift of real estate.

Disclosure statement A statement that explains possible risks of a planned-giving vehicle, given by the charity to the donor.

Dividends Payments made by corporations to shareholders based on the earnings of their stocks.

Donee A donee is the recipient of a charitable donation.

Dow Jones average This is the widely quoted stock average that is computed regularly and includes an industrial stock average, a transportation stock average, a utility average, and a combination of the three.

Endowment An endowment fund is a source of funds in perpetuity, whereby a distributable amount, e.g., 6 percent, may be distributed annually and the fund (and future distributions) continues to grow. Endowments are often restricted for specific purposes.

Estate tax A tax imposed on the transfer of assets. The most common is the federal estate tax collected by the IRS.

Executor The person named in a will to carry out the terms of the will and to settle the estate.

Face value The amount the issuing company of a bond will pay at maturity; it usually appears on the face of the bond.

Fair market value The value of an asset or property as determined by the price for which a seller will sell it and a buyer will pay for it.

Fiduciary   An individual or entity responsible for the management of assets for the benefit of others, including a trustee, executor, guardian, conservator, or a member of a board of directors.

Future interest   The interest of a beneficiary's right to use, enjoy, or possess that is postponed, as contrasted with a "present interest." The gift tax annual exclusion is not available for gifts of future interests.

Generation-skipping transfer tax   This tax is imposed when assets are transferred to grandchildren or to younger generations.

Gift tax   This tax is imposed on gifts made during lifetime. The unified transfer tax credit is available for gift taxes as well as for estate taxes. See **unified tax credit.**

Grantor   The individual who makes a gift.

Guardian   The person named in a will or appointed by the court to represent the interests of a minor child. A guardian of the person has legal custody of the minor, while the guardian of the estate is responsible for the minor's property.

Incident of ownership   An estate tax term that describes the ownership of a life insurance policy and whether the proceeds of that policy are to be included in the taxable estate.

Income beneficiary   The individual or charity who receives the income from a gift arrangement.

Income interest   The right to receive income from a trust.

Incomplete gift   A situation in which a gift is revocable or the donor has the opportunity to change the charitable beneficiary. This may affect the tax deductibility of the donation.

Individual Retirement Account   Also known as an IRA, this form of retirement plan is available to all working people under the age of 70½ who may contribute earned income of up to $2,000 to a qualified IRA account. Income tax is deferred until withdrawal (allowing for tax-free compounding), and the contribution amount is deducted from taxable income.

Insurable interest   This is the interest in a person's life that state law declares that the purchaser of insurance must have at the time the policy is purchased in order for the beneficiary to be entitled to receive the proceeds of the policy at the time of death. The rule is to prevent the gambling on the lives of others.

Inter vivos   Done during life, as opposed to testamentary, which is done at death.

Intestate   When an individual dies without a will. Probate courts will administer the assets owned by someone who dies intestate. The results are often undesirable.

Irrevocable gifts   These are gifts that cannot be changed or revoked.

Joint tenants   A person who co-owns a property with at least one other person. Their shares pass automatically to surviving joint tenants.

Legacy   Technically, a legacy is a bequest, but it is also used to describe a gift. When a donor makes a gift, he or she is leaving a legacy.

Liabilities   All the claims against a corporation, including accounts and wages and salaries payable, dividends declared payable, mortgages, debentures, and bank loans.

Lien   A claim against a property.

Life estate gift   A life estate gift includes life tenancies and life-income interests in trusts.

Life-income plan   Any charitable gift arrangement that pays out income to the donor, including a charitable gift annuity, a charitable remainder trust, or a pooled income fund.

Limited partnership   A partnership composed of one or more general partners willing to assume unlimited liability and limited partners who invest funds but are unwilling to assume unlimited liability. Their liability is generally limited to their investment in the partnership.

Liquid assets   These are assets that can be converted to cash quickly, including the cash value of life insurance, cash, and money in a checking or savings account.

Long-term capital gain   When an asset that has been owned for longer than one year has increased in value.

Marital deduction   Tax deduction allowed for estate and gift taxes for gifts made to spouses. This is the single most important deduction available to a married couple for reducing the tax on lifetime gifts or at death transfers. There is no limit on the size of this deduction. The only other unlimited deduction is the income tax charitable deduction.

Maturity   In investment terms, this refers to the date on which a loan or a bond or a debenture comes due and is to be paid off. In planned giving terms, some gifts "mature" when the donor dies.

NICRUT   The is an acronym for "net income charitable remainder unitrust," which is a trust arrangement whereby the payment made to the income beneficiaries is a set percentage but not more than the actual net accounting income of the trust.

NIMCRUT   This is an acronym for "net income charitable remainder unitrust with makeup provision." It refers to a trust arrangement whereby the payment made to the income beneficiaries is a set percentage of the fair market value of the trust, as revalued annually, but not more than the actual net accounting income. In any year in which the net accounting income exceeds the percentage amount, the trustee must "make up" for past deficits. This increases the payment made to the beneficiaries.

Paper profit   Profit on a security that only becomes realized when the stock is sold.

Partial interest   An interest in an asset that is less than the entire interest.

Percentage limitation   The percentage of a donor's income that he or she can claim as an income tax charitable deduction in any given year.

Personal property   Property other than real property, including books, art, jewelry, and other tangible items.

Present value   The value today of an amount to be paid in the future assuming certain interest rates. The amount that must be invested today at a specified interest rate in order to produce the specified amount at the specified time. Present value also depends on whether you assume simple or compound interest.

Principal   The body (corpus) of a fund; the amount of a bond.

Private annuity   An estate planning arrangement whereby children purchase assets from their parents in return for the unsecured promise to pay the parent a lifetime income. This arrangement lowers the parents' estate taxes.

Private foundation   Organizations that are created, funded, and operated by one person or a family, usually for grant-making purposes. These organizations may be formed as either corporations or trusts and are tax-exempt entities.

Probate   A court process to prove the validity of a will, to appoint executors, and to approve the executor's actions and accountings.

Prudent investor rule   This rule applies to trustees, executors, and other fiduciaries and mandates that they invest funds in adequately diversified portfolios of equity and debt instruments.

Qualified appreciated stock   Long-term capital gain stock of a corporation for which market quotations are available on an established stock market.

Qualified terminable interest property trust   Also called a QTIP trust, this is a marital deduction device in which the trustor spouse determines who the remainder beneficiaries will be. In regular marital deduction trusts, the beneficiary spouse can name or change the remainder beneficiaries. The estate tax or gift tax marital deduction for this trust must be elected in writing and is not automatic.

Quid pro quo   This refers to anything of value that is given in return for a donation. An example is when a donor gives an amount and receives a dinner, or a mug, or a membership valued at the same amount. The value of the quid pro quo reduces the donor's deduction.

Related use   In order for a donor to deduct the full fair market value of a gift of personal property, the gift must be related to the tax-exempt purpose of the charity. Donating books to a library fulfills the related use requirement, while a gift of livestock to a library would not constitute a related use.

Revocable trust   A trust in which a donor can revoke the trust before dying. A revocable trust becomes irrevocable at death or when a donor gives up the power to revoke. Other names for a revocable trust are a living trust or a family trust.

S corporation   Unlike a C corporation, an S corporation is not taxable, although the corporation's income is taxed to its shareholders. As of 1998 a nonprofit can hold stock in an S corporation; however a CRT cannot, or it will lose its charitable trust status. The nonprofit may be subject to some taxes on the S corporation stock, e.g., items of income, loss, credit or deduction, and any gain on the sale or disposition of the shares will flow through to the charity and will be included in computing unrelated business taxable income (UBTI).

Special needs trust   A trust designed to provide funds to care for a beneficiary's special needs so as not to disqualify the beneficiary from SSI (supplementary security income) or Medicaid coverage.

Spendthrift trust   A trust arrangement that disallows beneficiaries from assigning their interests and prevents the creditors of a beneficiary from taking the interest of the beneficiary. This arrangement can be a protection against personal injury lawsuits, divorce disputes, and catastrophic medical expenses, as well as the possibility of a spendthrift beneficiary who spends the trust's money too quickly.

Sprinkling or spray trusts   A trust arrangement that contains a provision giving the trustee the power to "sprinkle" income or "spray" capital in any manner. This arrangement would allow the trustee to distribute any part or all of the trust's income among beneficiaries in equal or unequal shares.

Stepped-up basis   The basis assets receive when they are includable in a decedent's estate for federal estate tax purposes. That basis is the fair market value of those assets on the date of death or the alternate valuation date (which is six months after the date of death).

Stock power   The assignment of the power to transfer stock on the books of a corporation.

Street name   Stocks held in the name of the broker rather than of the owner.

Testamentary   This refers to something written in a will.

Trustee   One or more individuals who administer and manage a trust. It can refer to a bank or a trust company as well.

Trustor   The individual who creates a trust and who places the assets in the trust. Usually it is the trustor who chooses the trustee(s) to administer and manage the trust.

Unified transfer tax credit A one-time credit available to all taxpayers that is sufficient to exempt an estate of $675,000 (2000). Current law provides that this credit will increase to $1 million in the year 2005 and beyond.

Unitrust This is another name for a charitable remainder unitrust, but could also refer to a charitable lead unitrust.

Unrelated business taxable income (UBTI) Income received by charities and charitable trusts on which the IRS imposes income taxes in spite of the tax-exempt status of the charity and charitable trust. UBTI is treated similarly to corporate income.

Will A written document with instructions for the disposition of assets and the naming of an executor, trustees, and guardians. The will may also establish trusts to be created and implemented at death.

BIBLIOGRAPHY

Abrams, Deborah B., and John S. Foster. "Solving the planned giving puzzle: You can piece together the gift vehicle that's just right for each prospect's needs—and yours." *Currents* 21, no. 3 (March 1995): 26–32.

This article highlights a reference chart developed at the University of Pennsylvania that covers a range of planned-giving vehicles including gift annuities, deferred gift annuities, pooled income fund, charitable remainder trusts, and a lead trust. The charts give concise information on suitable donors for each type of vehicle and features of each vehicle.

Adams, S. Charles. "In planned giving: Don't cook the meal, just serve it." *Fund Raising Management* 25, no. 12 (Feb. 1995): 14–17.

Planned giving need not be complicated, and Adams uses the metaphor of bringing friends to dinner but having a technician (or chef) prepare the meal. He stresses the importance of relationships and communication with prospects. The article does include tools of planned giving.

Aldrich, Daniel G. "A boom in baby-boom marketing?: A close-up look at one planned giving strategy for 30- and 40-somethings." *Currents* 20, no. 3 (March 1994): 26–29.

The author, an advancement professional at a newer school with younger alumni, gives practical information on starting a planned-giving program geared toward 30- to 40-year-olds. The program described relied on focus group information, volunteer experts, and a newsletter.

Anderson, Michael W. "Marketing planned gifts through a bequest society: Increasing the number of gifts for your charity—both outright and deferred—is the ultimate goal. A bequest society can advance that goal." *Fund Raising Management* 25, no. 12 (Feb. 1995): 28–30.

Identifying planned giving prospects is the first step to establishing a bequest society. The article continues with the practical steps for developing a bequest society including newsletters, events, and recognition.

Ashton, Deborah. *The Complete Guide to Planned Giving: Everything You Need to Know to Compete Successfully for Major Gifts.* Rev. ed. Cambridge, Mass.: JLA , 1991.

This large volume is divided into four categories: preparation for a planned-giving program, understanding gift options, running a successful planned-giving program, and essential resources. The book includes a bibliography, consultants, sample trust documents, and index.

———. "Why you don't get more gifts." *Planned Giving Today* 6, no. 12 (Dec. 1995): 1–2.

Ashton covers eleven suggestions for getting more planned gifts. These practical suggestions apply to the people skills involved in planned giving rather than the technical knowledge of gift vehicles.

Baxley, Eve B., and David J. Iommarini. "Marketing a planned giving program: Hitting a home run with a high-scoring, targeted approach." *Nonprofit Times* 9 (Sept. 1995): 38–39, 44.

The authors cover three important marketing principles for a successful direct mail planned-giving program: targeting, timing, and presenting the message. Targeting considerations include longevity of giving, frequency of giving, and the most important indicator: age. Summer is the worst time to do a mailing and fall is the most timely to feature income tax benefits. The article also emphasizes the importance of good cover letters to accompany a planned-giving brochure.

Bendixen, Mary Anne. "Planned giving on a shoestring budget." *Fund Raising Management* 22, no. 12 (Feb. 1992): 40.

The shoestring budget used in this article is upwards of $5,000 and the institution is a hospital in Los Angeles. However, the article has good advice on the use of newsletters and seminars and using volunteers and experts in the field.

Bingham, John. "The missing link for non-profit institutions." *Trusts & Estates* 137 (May 1998): 6.

Bingham discusses the need for software programs to take care of the administration of investments and charitable trusts. He also discusses external asset managers and bank trust departments.

Boedecker, Aviva S. "How to care for your donors." *Planned Giving Today* 6 (June 1995): 3–5.

A very practical approach to good stewardship of planned gift donors that includes thanking the donors, managing the gift, and properly reporting IRS requirements. Stewardship should continue so that additional gifts are more the rule than the exception. The article also gives practical information on condolences.

Bowen, William G. *Inside the Boardroom: Governance by Directors and Trustees*. New York: John Wiley, 1994.

Bowen's book covers all types of boards, not just nonprofit boards, and discusses corporate governance and the roles and responsibilities of corporate directors and trustees.

Burlingame, Dwight, ed. *Library Fundraising: Models for Success*. Chicago: American Library Association, 1995.

Contributors to this book are from a variety of libraries, and topics covered include special events, capital campaigns, and annual programs. A good basic source for library fund-raising but the index has no listing for planned giving.

Capek, Mary Ellen S. *Women and Philanthropy: Old Stereotypes, New Challenges*. St. Paul, Minn.: Women's Funding Network.

This monograph series is published by The Women's Funding Network. This issue is currently out of print but will be re-released by the Kellogg Foundation. The three monographs in this series provide an overview of philanthropy as it affects women and girls.

Caswell, Gordon M. "A life and death issue: Understanding mortality concerns can give fundraisers a greater measure of compassion and intuition as they assist donors with planned or testamentary gifts." *Fund Raising Management* 26, no. 12 (1996) 28–29.

In this first-person narrative the author discusses the difficult decision to plan one's own funeral and the sensitivity it gave him as a development professional when assisting donors with planned or testamentary gifts.

Christensen, Burke A. "Back to the basics: Estate planning for the layman." *Trusts & Estates* 136, no. 7 (June 1997): 61–63.

Discusses estate planning as it pertains to tax planning and directing assets.

———. "The wisdom of deferring estate taxes. (Response to Jeffrey N. Pennell and R. Mark Williamson)" *Trusts & Estates* 136, no. 9 (June 1997): 67–69.

Burke disputes the assertion that it is better to pay estate taxes before death and discusses the marital deduction to defer estate taxes.

Clough, Leonard G., David G. Clough, Ellen G. Estes, and Ednalou C. Ballard. *Practical Guide to Planned Giving.* Detroit: Taft Group, 1998.

This highly recommended and excellent guide to planned giving contains a plethora of forms and resource lists.

Connell, James E. "Communicating charitable estate planning to older adults." *AHP Journal* (spring 1997): 29–32.

Connell makes the important point that development professionals must listen carefully to better understand the financial and personal needs of older prospects because they are quite a diverse group.

Converse, P. "Think of the possibilities! Most people have the capability and the willingness to give substantially more at death than during their lifetime, thanks to planned giving." *Fund Raising Management* 21, no. 12 (Feb. 1991): 54.

Converse asserts that bequests can generate more income for nonprofits than corporate and foundation gifts and that most people have the capability to give substantially more at death than during their lifetime. These are two major factors in establishing a planned-giving program even though the rewards come later.

Dean, James C. "Development dynamics (model of relationship between planned giving, major gifts, and annual giving)." *Fund Raising Management* 29, no. 1 (March 1998): 9–13.

Dean provides a new model of the relationship between planned giving, major gifts, and annual giving.

Dewey, B., ed. *Raising Money for Academic and Research Libraries.* New York: Neal-Schuman, 1991.

This volume is part of the How-to-Do-It Manuals for Libraries published by Neal-Schuman. Chapters cover the basics: development plans, Friends, donor relations, grants, corporations, campaigns, planned giving, public relations, and development personnel. Many contributors are or were members of DORAL (Development Officers of Research Academic Libraries).

Eiseman, Cynthia Jones. "Value added: Donor advised funds at community foundations." *Trusts & Estates* 136, no. 4 (March 1997): 16–20.

Eiseman discusses donor advised funds at community foundations and compares them with private foundations and commercial organizations, such as Fidelity Investments.

Ellentuck, Albert B. "Maximizing the charitable contribution deduction when donating tangible personal property." *Tax Advisor* 26, no. 3 (March 1995): 180–181.

This article covers the related purpose issues of donations of tangible personal property.

Fagan, P. J. *Charitable Remainder Trusts: A Proven Strategy for Reducing Estate and Income Taxes through Charitable Giving.* Burr Ridge, Ill.: Irwin, 1996.

The author, a financial planner, attempts to demystify charitable trusts and, in particular, charitable remainder trusts. He emphasizes CRTs as vehicles for converting individual financial situations that are negative into positive financial situations and considers options and issues for both donors and charities.

Hamilton, Charles H., and Warren R. Ilchman. *Cultures of Giving II: How Heritage, Gender, Wealth, and Values Influence Philanthropy.* San Francisco: Jossey-Bass, 1995.

This collection of essays is a part of the Jossey-Bass series on non-profits and covers giving by regions and religions.

Hargroves, Gary G. "How to prepare for your next visit." *Planned Giving Today* 6 (Dec. 1995): 3–4.

The author covers setting and achieving goals for personal visits to prospects and donors. The sequential process covers gathering personal information, financial information, qualifying the donor, clarifying objectives, preparing proposals, involving advisors, closing the gift, attending to records and recognition.

Hartsook, Robert F. "Top ten solicitation mistakes." *Fund Raising Management* 28, no. 1 (March 1997): 48.

Hartsook covers the most common mistakes that fund-raisers make when soliciting donations, including not listening, not asking, not following up, and failing to come up with a strategy for individual donors.

Horowitz, Steven A. "Charitable planned giving." *Taxes: The Tax Magazine* 72, no. 11 (Nov. 1994): 685–696.

This long article goes into great technical detail on the charitable remainder trust and the charitable lead trust.

Jensen, John W. "Marketing planned giving." *Non-Profit Times* 11, no. 4 (March 1997): 46–48.

The basic premise of this article is to market your planned-giving program to the right people, and the most relevant information you can have is the donor's age. The author gives useful information for database maintenance and pertinent demographics.

Jordan, Ronald R., and Katelyn L. Quynn. "Material benefits: From basic to deluxe, the publications every planned giving program needs." *Currents* 18, no. 3 (March 1992): 26–33.

The authors of this article have also written the highly useful and practical book *Planned Giving: Management, Marketing, and Law.*

This article covers the materials a planned-giving program needs to be successful from basic to deluxe. The emphasis is on practical and informative publications.

————. *Planned Giving: Management, Marketing, and Law*. New York: John Wiley, 1994.

A well-organized and highly useful book, providing a range of information on planned giving including building a planned-giving program, marketing, planned-giving assets, deferred gifts, related disciplines, and planned giving in context. It includes a disk with templates of relevant forms, letters, and gift vehicles.

Kley, Carolyn, George Schmelzie, and Ira Greenberg. "Maximizing the tax advantages of charitable giving." *Michigan CPA* 46, no. 2 (fall 1994): 26–27.

This short article covers the provisions in the Internal Revenue Code that provide significant deductions on income tax, gift tax, and estate tax returns.

Kling, Paul F., and H. Gerald Quigg. "Integrating a planned giving program." *Fund Raising Management* 27, no. 4 (June 1996): 32–40.

The authors contend that planned-giving programs will be more productive by integrating efforts to various sectors of your nonprofit. An example is alumni affairs.

Lee, H., and G. A. Hunt. *Fundraising for the 1990s: The Challenge Ahead: A Practical Guide for Library Fundraising, from Novice to Expert*. Canfield, Ohio: Genawa, 1992.

Three pages of this book are devoted to planned giving with bulleted paragraphs on planned-giving vehicles: bequests, life insurance, pooled income funds, charitable remainder trusts, charitable lead trusts, and charitable annuity and uniterm trusts.

Lee, Susan, and Christine Foster. "A how-to-give primer." *Forbes* 160, no. 13 (Dec. 15, 1997): 84–86.

The authors cover donor-advised funds, charitable remainder trusts, pooled income funds, endowment funds, charitable lead trusts, and private foundations, cash gifts, and appreciated property.

Logan, F. A. "Planned giving." In Deni Elliott, *Ethics of Asking: Dilemmas in Higher Education Fund Raising.* Baltimore, Md.: Johns Hopkins University Press, 1995.

The basic premise of this chapter is that planned giving differs from other institutional advancement in that it emphasizes service, not salesmanship and problem solving, not promotion. The chapter further discusses contractual agreements, ethical issues, model standards, and enforcement.

Mann, Barlow T. "Are your donors in the market for planned gifts? Today's economic environment provides powerful incentives for donors to plan their current and deferred gifts in the most effective manner possible." *Fund Raising Management* 26, no. 12 (Feb. 1996): 31–33.

Today's economic environment, including the upward trend of the Dow Jones Industrial Average, provides a powerful incentive for donors to give. Mann gives examples of strategies and alternatives that will benefit donors with great wealth.

Mannix, Margaret. "A how-to guide for the serious giver: of trusts, pooled income, and foundations." *U.S. News and World Report* 123 (Dec. 22, 1997): 75–76.

This brief article describes methods of giving including securities, gift funds, foundations, trusts, and pooled income funds.

Martin, Gary J. "Thanks in advance: How recognizing planned gifts can help get more and bigger donations." *Currents* 16, no. 5 (May 1990): 22–26.

The emphasis of this article is on organizing a planned-giving recognition program with comparisons of five different established programs, as well as information on the author's heritage club at Texas A&M.

McBride, Edward J. "Advisory board primer." *Planned Giving Today* 6 (Jan. 1995): 5–6.

The author presents practical, concise information on a planned-giving advisory board including a plan, the mission, frequency and length of meetings, membership, site location, chairs, and agendas.

Miree, Kathryn W. "How to involve professional advisors." *Planned Giving Today* 6, no. 5 (May 1995): 1–9.

This very practical article covers why you should include professional advisors, which professional advisors, why professional advisors want to serve, and advisors on your board of trustees or advisory board.

Moerschbaecher, Lynda S. *Start at Square One: Starting and Managing the Planned Gift Program.* Chicago: Precept Pr., 1998.

Moerschbaecher, a planned-giving guru, outlines the necessary steps for developing a comprehensive planned-giving program.

Moran, William J. "Planned giving: Wealth is not a prerequisite." *Fund Raising Management* 22, no. 12 (Feb. 1992): 22–23, 58.

Assets, not wealth, are prerequisites for planned giving. The author outlines a profile of a planned giver: assets, record of involvement, age, and no heirs. He also further outlines those who have an interest in life income agreements.

———. "Solving the puzzle of planned giving." *Fund Raising Management* 24, no. 12 (Feb. 1994): 14.

Moran seeks to define planned giving and to clarify basic and confusing concepts. This article is helpful for dubious boards who are leery of committing scarce resources for a long period when the results, or gifts, are deferred. Moran stresses the need for long-term relationships with donors.

Newman, David Wheeler, and Reynolds T. Cafferata. "Charitable gifts of retirement plan assets." *Fund Raising Management* 26, no. 1 (March 1995): 38–41.

Newman and Cafferata are well known in the planned-giving field as the experts on the use of retirement plan assets for charitable gifts.

Peters, Robert F. R. Jr. "Ten key strategies to securing a bequest." *Fund Raising Management* 26, no. 1 (Feb. 1996): 44–47.

This article contains highly practical information on establishing and running a successful bequest solicitation program. The article is geared toward small to mid-size development programs.

Planned Giving for the One-Person Development Office: Taking the First Steps. 2nd ed. Wheaton, Ill.: Deferred Giving Services, 1994.

This book in a binder is a step-by-step account of how to set up a planned-giving program and covers marketing plan, recruiting board members, compiling a mailing list, preparing a budget, newsletters, recognition programs, capital campaigns, gift clubs, and endowment funds. The book also contains examples, a glossary of terms, and a bibliography.

Polisher, Edward N., and Charles Bender. "Appointing a CRUT as retirement plan beneficiary." *Trusts & Estates* 135, no. 8 (July 1996): 16–20.

This article examines the charitable remainder unitrust (CRUT) as a retirement plan beneficiary since it avoids many taxes.

Prince, Russ Alan, and Karen Maru File. *The Seven Faces of Philanthropy.* San Francisco: Jossey-Bass, 1994.

The authors discuss the seven types of donors and how to cultivate them. The seven profiles include the Communitarian, the Devout, the Investor, the Socialite, the Altruist, the Repayer, and the Dynast.

Reis, George. "The 1997 non-profit software directory." *Fund Raising Management* 27, no. 8 (Oct. 1996): 12–23.

Lists and discusses software designed for nonprofits.

Reiss, Alvin. "Library raises $34 million by focusing on big donors." *Fund Raising Management* 27, no. 4 (June 1996): 52–55.

The article discusses the successful campaign by the Frick Art Reference Library in New York City, which raised $34 million.

Rothblatt, Daniel. "Integrating major gifts and planned giving." *Fund Raising Management* 26, no. 3 (May 1995): 28–30.

This article discusses the integration of major gifts with planned giving, covering marketing, identification, cultivation, and solicitation.

Ruser, Katherine, and Sheran Fernando, eds. *Practical Guide to Planned Giving.* Rockville, Md.: Taft Group, 1996.

Practical is the operative word for this large volume, although comprehensive would apply as well. This guide begins with information on feasibility studies and covers setting up a planned-giving program, implementing, marketing, and use of consultants. Section III covers planned-giving devices, including revocable vehicles, nontrust irrevocable vehicles, irrevocable trusts, and types of gift properties. The last section covers tax and financial implications. The volume also includes extensive appendixes.

Saunders, Laura. "Doing well by doing good." *Forbes* 154, no. 10 (Oct. 24, 1994): 106–108.

Saunders discusses making a bequest from an IRA, which lowers estate taxes while making a charitable contribution.

———. "The donated IRA: Is this a good time to make a charitable gift or bequest from your retirement assets? Study the tax arithmetic before making your move." *Forbes* 159, no. 6 (March 24, 1997): 182–184.

This article discusses the strategy of using retirement plans for charitable giving.

Schoenhals, G. R. *On My Way in Planned Giving: Inspiring Anecdotes and Advice for Gift-Planning Professionals.* Seattle, Wash.: Planned Giving Today, 1995.

Schoenhals is the editor and publisher of *Planned Giving Today,* and this book is a compilation of "On My Way" columns that he wrote. The stories are short, entertaining, and insightful.

Sharpe, Robert F. "Starting on the right foot." *Planned Giving Today* 6, no. 5 (May 1995).

Planning is the first step to establishing a planned-giving program. The author covers 11 items that must be addressed before communicating the planned-giving concept to donors.

Shaw, Sondra C. and Martha A. Taylor. *Reinventing Fundraising: Realizing the Potential of Women's Philanthropy.* San Francisco: Jossey-Bass, 1995.

Another entry in the Jossey-Bass nonprofit series, this volume covers women philanthropists and is an important contribution to this emerging area of importance in fund-raising.

Smith, Thomas W. "Little things mean a lot." *Currents* 23, no. 3 (March 1997): 40–44.

This article gives practical advice on marketing your planned-giving program without the benefit of a big budget.

Steele, Victoria, and Steven D. Elder. *Becoming a Fundraiser.* 2nd ed. Chicago: American Library Association, 2000.

Victoria Steele is the guru of academic library development, and she and Steve Elder have written a comprehensive book on the principles and practice of library development. The book includes a short section within a chapter on planned giving that gives basic and easy-to-follow technical information on planned-giving prospects.

Sullivan, J. Craig. "Achieving immortality on the installment plan— using life insurance to donate to charity." *Best's Review—Life Health Insurance Edition* 96 (Aug. 1995): 72.

The author discusses how life insurance policies can be used to make charitable contributions.

Teitell, C. *Portable Planned Giving Manual.* Rev. ed. Old Greenwich, Conn.: Taxwise Giving, 1993.

This hefty volume is organized and reads like a law book; it does not appear to be very "portable" after all. The manual is based on the Internal Revenue Code, treasury regulations, and revenue rulings as of August 15, 1993, and includes discussions of the relevant provisions of the Omnibus Budget Reconciliation Act of 1993. Highly technical.

Vimuktanon, Atisaya. "Non-profits and the Internet." *Fund Raising Management* 28, no. 8 (Oct. 1997): 25–29.

This article covers the Internet as a fund-raising tool, including e-mail, electronic discussion lists, and Web sites. Includes noteworthy sites and addresses.

White, Douglas E. *The Art of Planned Giving: Understanding Donors and the Culture of Giving.* New York: John Wiley, 1995.

According to the author, this book is written for anyone whose interest in planned giving is beyond the technical and flows from philosophical to personal to technical to organizational to ethical.

Zabel, William D. "Healthy, wealthy, and taxwise." *Town and Country* 149 (March 1995): 40–45.

Zabel explains the tax benefits of charitable giving in layman's language.

INDEX

Amy Sherman Smith received her MS in Library Services from Columbia University in 1977. Currently, she is the director of development for the College of Humanities, Arts, and Social Sciences at the University of California, Riverside.

Matthew D. Lehrer is a consultant and attorney who works with nonprofit groups to establish new planned-giving programs. He also provides assistance in structuring gifts and gift administration. He has authored professional newsletters, edited a planned-giving handbook for professional advisors, and served as a panelist and speaker for presentations to both professional and lay audiences.